ADVENT ANTICIPATION:
DRAWING NEARER TO THE CHRIST-CHILD

ADVENT ANTICIPATION:
DRAWING NEARER TO THE CHRIST-CHILD

JEANNE CONTE

TROITSA BOOKS
Huntington, NY

Editorial Production: Susan Boriotti
Office Manager: Annette Hellinger
Graphics: Frank Grucci and Jennifer Lucas
Information Editor: Tatiana Shohov
Book Production: Patrick Davin, Cathy DiGregory, Donna Dennis, Jennifer Kuenzig,
　　　　　　　　Christine Mathosian, Tammy Sauter and Lynette Van Helden
Circulation: Lisa DiGangi and Michael Pazy Mino

Library of Congress Cataloging-in-Publication Data

Conte, Jeanne
　　Advent anticipation: drawing nearer to the Christ-child / by Jeanne Conte.
　　p.cm.
　　ISBN 1-56072-741-1.
　　1. Advent—Prayer-books and devotions—English. 2. Christmas—Prayer-books and devotions—English. I. Title

BV40 .C57 1999
242'.322—dc21

　　　　　　　　　　　　　　　　　　　　　　　　　　　　　　　　99-051396

Copyright © 2000 by Jeanne Conte
　　　　　　Troitsa Books, a division of
　　　　　　Nova Science Publishers, Inc.
　　　　　　227 Main Street, Suite 100
　　　　　　Huntington, New York 11743
　　　　　　Tele. 631-424-6682　　　Fax 631-424-4666
　　　　　　E Mail Novascil@aol.com

All rights reserved. No part of this book may be reproduced, stored in a retrieval system or transmitted in any form or by any means: electronic, electrostatic, magnetic, tape, mechanical photocopying, recording or otherwise without permission from the publishers.

The authors and publisher have taken care in preparation of this book, but make no expressed or implied warranty of any kind and assume no responsibility for any errors or omissions. No liability is assumed for incidental or consequential damages in connection with or arising out of information contained in this book.

This publication is designed to provide accurate and authoritative information with regard to the subject matter covered herein. It is sold with the clear understanding that the publisher is not engaged in rendering legal or any other professional services. If legal or any other expert assistance is required, the services of a competent person should be sought. FROM A DECLARATION OF PARTICIPANTS JOINTLY ADOPTED BY A COMMITTEE OF THE AMERICAN BAR ASSOCIATION AND A COMMITTEE OF PUBLISHERS.

Printed in the United States of America

Catholic Diocese of Columbus

Office of the Bishop
614-224-2251

May 28, 1999

Ms. Jeanne Conte
1469 Kenwick Road
Columbus, Ohio 43209

Dear Ms. Conte:

By means of this letter, and after recommendation of our censor deputatis Msgr. John Wolf, I am happy to grant to your two works, titled (1) Advent Anticipation: Drawing Nearer to the Christ-Child and (2) Lenten Reflections: A Closer Walk, the necessary imprimatur that works such as these would require.

You must state with the imprimatur that the imprimatur means that the works are considered free from doctrinal error and do not necessarily reflect the opinion of the person granting the imprimatur.

Again, I thank you for making these wonderful works available to the Catholic faithful, as well as to other interested Christians.

Please be assured of my prayers as we approach these summer months.

With every best wish, I am

Sincerely in Christ,
James A. Griffin
Bishop of Columbus

CONTENTS

FOREWORDS	ix
PREFACE AND APPRECIATIONS	xiii
COPYRIGHT ACKNOWLEDGMENTS	xv
PART I	1
Chapter 1: Advent Season: The Nativity Lent	3
Chapter 2: How to Use this Little Book	9
PART II	13
Chapter 3: Forty Daily Readings for Advent	15
PART III	77
Chapter 4: Christmas Eve and the Twelve Days of Christmas	79
REFERENCES/ENDNOTES	107

FOREWORDS

The excellent meditations found throughout *Advent Anticipation: Drawing Nearer to the Christ-Child*, by Jeanne Conte, offer the reader an opportunity to prepare for the celebration of Christmas through the unique ecumenical perspective of both Eastern and Western Christian traditions. The concepts presented offer insightful glimpses of God's Covenant (both Old and New) with humanity as He allowed the Divine Nature of the Word of God to condescend in taking on a Human Nature in the Person of our Lord and Saviour Jesus Christ.

This display of God's compassionate, disinterested benevolence, so well expressed throughout the prayers, poetry, Biblical Readings, hymnals and inspirational writings found in this book, help the reader to experience a meaningful pre-Christmas preparation which uplifts the soul while allowing thoughtful contemplation of God's magnificent outpouring of divine love. Ms. Conte then takes the reader to a celebration of this great Feast of the Nativity that continues through to "little Christmas" and Epiphany. The insightful message of God's love permeates this book in an encouraging way that will help to enliven the reader's spiritual life in Christ.

The Rev. Dr. Athanasios Demos, Pastor
St. George Greek Orthodox Church
Bethesda, Maryland USA

This 'little book', as the author calls it, contains far more depth than its physical size suggests. As Christians, we approach Christmas from so many different traditions and calendars which can drive us apart at the very time of year we should be celebrating together. I believe that this little book will give the reader an insight into what Advent means to other Christians and will thereby heighten the anticipation of 'Christ-come-to-us'. In season, the scriptures and meditations here will warm your heart, broaden your thinking and help you keep the true meaning of Advent and Christmas in perspective. Out of season there are depths here into which you can dip and be refreshed in your daily journey with God.

Pastor Peter Kelsall
Youth Activities Director
Aldridge Methodist Church
Walsall, UK

One of the dictionary meanings for "devotion" is "deep affection." In this devotional book, Jeanne Conte projects clearly her own deep affection for the Christ child born at Christmas. Through hymns, poems, Scripture readings, and prayers, she allows her deep affection for Jesus to draw in her readers, even as she draws on resources from many centuries and many different Christian faith traditions.

In her prayer for the Fourteenth Day of Advent, the author reveals one of the goals of her study: "O Lord God, ... help us to establish within ourselves the qualities of Isaac -- meditation, affection, peaceableness and prayerfulness." Jesus, she writes often, is a gift. So is this book. The book provides the structure for its readers to meditate, to express their affection for the baby born at Christmas, to enter into the peace of God, and to pray.

Those who invest a few moments each day will find this book a gift that will enrich their Advent preparations and Christmas celebrations.

Rev. Walter F. Taylor, Ph.D.
Ernest W. and Elizabeth S. Ogram Professor
of New Testament Studies
Trinity Lutheran Seminary
Columbus, Ohio USA

This little book is unusual and distinctive in its ecumenical character, and its Christian readers will find in its pages a source of spiritual inspiration for the observance of the seasons of Advent and Christmas. Its author Jeanne Conte has compiled an impressive collection of quotations from Holy Scripture, historic and contemporary prayers, religious poetry, hymns and carols, and her own relevant commentary. She has created a devotional manual acceptable to all Christians who celebrate the anticipatory season of Advent and the joyful season of Christmas.

At Advent the anticipation can be joyful and expectant as we look forward and seek to "prepare the way of the Lord." This anticipation should also be a reminder of "the last day" when Jesus "shall come again in glorious majesty to judge both the living and the dead."

At Christmas the joy of the Incarnation of God in the Person of Jesus Christ fills our hearts. This joy should be unbounded as all Christians celebrate the feast of Our Lord's Nativity when "the Word became flesh."

I commend this book to all Christians who seek to know the Saving Person of the Lord Jesus and His Kingdom which touches our daily lives. May the season of Advent fill your hearts and minds with anticipation, and may the season of Christmas fill you with joy and wonder.

Fr. Jeffrey Martin Richards
Retired Priest
Episcopal Church
Akron, Ohio USA

Searching is part of the Christian vocation and commitment. Sometimes exciting, usually difficult, often painful, the search is part of the life of Jesus' followers. But sometimes when others have gone before us in their own searches, we can benefit from their explorations and profit from their discoveries as we follow our similar paths.

Jeanne Conte has searched faithfully and resolutely for her God through reading, poetry, reflection, research, study, travel, discussion, and especially through her own questioning and prayer. On her own journey, delving into texts and places where most of us will never venture personally, she has caught glimpses of her God, and she has talked with others who view God with different eyes--or even view a different god. These booklets give us access to what she has found.

One of the first things that strikes the reader is the breadth and depth of the resources the booklets offer. They are extremely well-researched and provide a wealth of interesting detail and insight that help us see Advent and Lent in a new light and from different perspectives.

Particularly interesting are the notes that Jeanne offers about the various authors and hymn writers and poets she quotes. The work of familiar writers takes on new meaning when we learn about their background or a family connection, and the notes also help us to become acquainted with and appreciate other writers previously unknown.

In their approach, the booklets do not impose a rigid, one-size-fits-all regime for the Christian seriously entering into these special seasons but rather they offer encouragement to make our Advent or Lenten journey a deeply personal spiritual experience.

Jeanne offers a variety of ideas, insights, and options to help the reader accomplish this. The booklets contain an intriguing mix of scripture, poetry, prayer, history, liturgy, and culture, and these various elements build upon and call attention to each other. And together they become a foundation on which Jeanne constructs her own thoughtful reflections which she offers as a guide in the search for Jesus in the world today.

Advent and Lent are very old, very traditional parts of the church's liturgical year. The task and challenge of the church and the individual Christian is to make them new and motivating each year. Jeanne Conte's texts and reflections encourage and assist us to do just that.

The Reverend Father Charles Dittmeier
Roman Catholic Priest
Maryknoll Missionary to the deaf in Cambodia and Hong Kong

PREFACE AND APPRECIATIONS

It has been a deep blessing gathering this book together, immersing myself in the holy Word and His people across time and place. I'm deeply troubled by dissension among we who call ourselves Christians. Jesus' words: *" ... that all of them may be one, Father, just as you are in me and I am in you. ... that the world may believe that you have sent me,"* (John 17:21) ring in my ears and are a reason for this little book which crosses denominational barriers, uniting us in His love. I asked members of the clergy from different Christian traditions for brief forewords, and was taken aback by their kind praise. But then I realized that this was, of course, praise for God Who is the giver of every good gift. There is nothing I can do without Him; any good in these books is simply a reflection of our Lord God. So I offer my deep appreciation for all who made this possible, first, of course, my Maker -- the triune Creator God. Then I thank my patient publishers, Mr. & Mrs. Frank and Nadya Columbus, and my friends: Christo J. Balouris, James Bergeron, Michael Bishop and his website (http.//www.Michael-Bishop.com/), Rev. Dr. Athanasios Demos, Rev. Father Charles Dittmeier, Bishop James Griffin, Pastor Peter Kelsall, Nicolas Luco, Bishop Alexander Mileant and his website (http://www.fatheralexander.org /index.html), Very Rev. Father Jeffrey Richards, Philip Tamoush, Rev. Dr. Walter Taylor, Rev. Father Philip Vreelend, Keith Wakefield, Rev. Father Robert Willmann, Msgr. John Wolf, the many publishers who offered use of their works, my supportive husband, Joe, and you, the reader, without whom this would never have been possible.

COPYRIGHT ACKNOWLEDGMENTS

I gratefully acknowledge the kindness of the following for permission for the use of their copyrighted works:

Catholic Book Publishing Company: for excerpts from THE SAINT JOSEPH DAILY MISSAL Copyright (c) 1959, Catholic Book Publishing Company, New York, New York; all rights reserved.

International Bible Society: Scripture taken from THE HOLY BIBLE, NEW INTERNATIONAL VERSION. Copyright (c) 1973, 1978, 1984 by International Bible Society. All rights reserved.

John Murray (Publishers), Ltd.: excerpt from poem "Christmas," by John Betjeman, from *COLLECTED POEMS*, Houghton Mifflin, Boston. Copyright (c) 1970. All rights reserved.

Oakwood Publications, Philip Tamoush, Publisher: for permission to use excerpts from AWAKE TO LIFE, (trans. Marite Sapiets) Copyright (c) 1996, and SON OF MAN, (trans. Samuel Brown) Copyright (c) 1999. All rights reserved.

Samuel Brown, translator: for permission for the use of excerpts from SON OF MAN, copyright (c) 1999; all rights reserved.

Society of Jesus of New England: for excerpts from HANDBOOK OF CHRISTIAN FEASTS AND CUSTOMS, by Francis X. Weiser, (c) 1958; all rights reserved.

Stainer & Bell, Ltd., administered by Hope Publishing Company: words to carol "The Holly and the Ivy" by Emily Chisholm, from HYMNS & PSALMS, The Methodist Publishing House (c) 1983. All rights reserved.

"The virgin ... will give birth to a son, and they will call him 'Immanuel' -- which means, 'God with us.'" (1)

Matthew 1: 22 & 23
(c) International Bible Society 1984

"For God so loved the world that he gave his one and only Son, that whoever believes in him shall not perish but have eternal life."
John 3: 16

Part I

Chapter 1

ADVENT SEASON: THE NATIVITY LENT

"I have come that they may have life, and have it to the full."
John 10:10

Advent -- that time of awesome anticipation -- the weeks just before Christmas -- is many things to many people. Called Nativity Fast or Nativity Lent in the East, its observance varies widely in tradition. It is, however, to all Christendom, the time of preparation for the celebration of Christ's coming into the world long ago as a tiny baby in Bethlehem.

The season offers an effort at penitence, but always with an undercurrent of great joy. *"... partly a time of joy and partly a time of mournful penance,"* (2) was the way William Duranti, Bishop of Ravenna, spoke of it in the year 1296. We *can* be penitent and we *can* be fully forgiven, and be surrounded by peace and joy thanks to the great-grand Love manifest at Christmas.

The word Advent is from Old French or Latin; it signifies the coming of an event of extreme importance. The Latin word adventus (or advenhre) can be broken down to "ad" meaning "adding," and "ventus" meaning "come." Actually, the custom of a penitential preparation season before Christmas appears to have begun in Gaul. Hence, the Old French derivation of the word Advent.

In the year 490, Bishop Perpetuus of Tours issued directions for his people to fast three days each week from November 11, St. Martin's feast day, until Christmas. Known as Quadragesima Sancti Martini (Forty Days Fast of St. Martin), it resembled in both time and duration the current continuing observation of the Orthodox Churches today. Both spread from mid-November until Christmas, and both are called by the name of the saint whose day is celebrated at the beginning of their observance -- St. Martin in ancient Gaul, and St. Philip for the Eastern churches today.

Christmas Lent is another name given to this season of Nativity Fast in the East which lasts forty days, beginning on November 15, St. Philip's Day (St. Philip's Fast), and ending on Christmas Eve. Observed by all but the infirm, elderly or very young, it is a penitential season -- a serious and solemn fast as well as a time of alms-giving and a time of meaningful services.

So, also, the Coptic Christians of Egypt observe a solemn season of stringent fasting during Advent. This is at least a forty day plus a week fast until January 6 when Christmas is celebrated as a major and most joyous Eide (festival). Armenian Christians fast during their Advent season spreading from mid-November until Epiphany.

In the Middle East, the Holy Lands where Jesus walked, the Advent season is filled with services during which prayers are fervently offered for the poor; many baskets of food are prepared and given to them, often with carefully saved money, especially during the week of Christmas.

In Western churches Advent begins four Sundays before Christmas, technically on the Sunday nearest November 30 -- St. Andrew's Day. This is usually, in the United States, the Sunday immediately following Thanksgiving. Also in the Western observance, four different ways that Christ comes are symbolized by the four weeks of Advent: 1) in His birth on earth; 2) in the hearts of believers; 3) at death; and 4) on Judgment Day.

The Advent Wreath symbolizes the divine portent of these four weeks in the four candles encircled by evergreen. Both the evergreens and the circle represent eternity -- life without end through the gift of the Christ-Child. Its candles represent the light our Savior brings into the darkness. In Jesus' words:

"I am the Light of the world. Whoever follows me will never walk in darkness, but will have the light of life."

John 8: 12

In some traditions, especially in various Christian denominations in England, the wreath is of holly and ivy and four red candles are placed within its greenery, with a white one in the center. The liturgy is closely associated with the ancient carol, "The Holly and the Ivy," yet with rather recent 20th century words by Emily Chisholm. Each Sunday in Advent, candles are lit. The first week, one red candle is lit along with readings about the faithfull witness of the church; then the first two verses of the carol are sung. The second Sunday, a second red candle is lit as Old Testament prophesies about Jesus are read, then the first three verses of the carol are sung. The fourth week, three red candles are lit with readings about the annunciation and Mary, as the first five verses of the carol are sung. On Christmas Day, all candles are lit and the complete carol sung.

In other traditions, especially in the United States within the Roman Catholic, Lutheran and Episcopal churches, during the daily Advent Wreath observance (usually in the home at dinner-time), the youngest child present normally lights the first candle the first week -- a purple candle representing penitence; the eldest child present lights the second purple candle during the second week's observance; the third week, beginning with Gaudete (joyful) Sunday, the mother lights the pink candle (for what Christian can contain joy during Advent?); and, throughout the fourth week, the father lights the fourth candle -- purple. In some traditions, a family member with the name of John, Joan or Jean lights the first candle, symbolizing the fore-runner John the Baptist. On Christmas day, the wreath is filled with all white candles to be lit on each of the twelve days of Christmas.

Another common custom is the Advent Log -- a real log in which holes are drilled to hold twenty-eight candles -- one to be lit on each day of Advent. Again, purple candles are used in an effort to remind us to "repent and prepare the way ... " as John enjoined. Pink candles are sometimes interspersed among the purple candles for use on Sundays. Finally, on Christmas Eve, the entire Yule Log is burned and as it is lit, the following prayer may be said:

> *"Oh holy Lord, as this Yule Log burns and vanishes into smoke and ash, may all our old hatreds, misunderstandings and envies vanish, too. Please purge us of our sins, and let the spirit of good fellowship reign among all, throughout this season and during all the coming year. Amen."*

Because Christmas falls on a different day each year, the fourth week of Advent, in the Western tradition, is never finished; it is interrupted suddenly and joyously with the symbolic coming again of Christ at Christmas, just as we are always in the Advent-time of Christ's second coming which will also one day be joyously interrupted with the sudden second coming of our Lord.

The purpose of this book is an attempt to help us draw nearer to Jesus during the holy season of His birth. The daily readings bear heavily on the prophecies of the Old Testament which point to the Redeemer-Child.

During these busy and oft-hectic days of preparation for Jesus' birthday -- in the West, the festive time of garlands, tinsel, gift-gathering, sweets-baking, and parties -- in the East, a penitential time of serious fasting, yet with an immersion into feelings of deep happiness -- may a few daily moments with this little book enable us to draw nearer to the Christ-Child Himself, allowing us the wonder and grace of being touched by His presence.

THE HOLLY AND THE IVY (3)

The holly and the ivy
Are dancing in a ring,
Round the berry-bright red candles
And the white and shining King.

Oh, one is for God's people
In every age and day.
We are watching for his coming.
We believe and we obey.

And two is for the prophets
And for the light they bring.
They are candles in the darkness,
All alight for Christ the King.

And three for John the Baptist.
He calls on us to sing:
O prepare the way for Jesus Christ,
He is coming, Christ the King.

And four for Mother Mary.
I cannot see the way,
But you promise me a baby.
I believe you. I obey.
And Christ is in the centre,

For this is his birthday,
With the shining nights of Christmas singing:
He has come today!

Emily Chisholm[1]
(c) Stainer & Bell, Ltd.
All rights reserved

---

[1] Emily Chisholm, 20th century theologian, poet, teacher and translator, was head of modern languages at a school in Essex, England. Her version of THE HOLLY AND THE IVY has become widely used for accompaniment to the Advent wreath tradition.

Chapter 2

How to Use this Little Book

It is hoped that this little book will be useful for any and all who may be looking for a way, by spending a few moments of each day, to draw nearer to the Christ-Child during the high-holy time of the year when we look forward once again to the celebration of the birth of Jesus in Bethlehem.

Realizing there are vast differences in traditions and even calendars among those who follow Christ, we've arrived at a means of making this usable, hopefully, to all who follow Him, whether they call the season prior to Jesus' birthday Advent, Nativity Fast, Christmas Lent or by any other name.

What unites us as Christians is infinitely more than anything that separates us; it is Jesus Christ Himself, our Lord and Savior.

About this, He once said:

"A new command I give you: Love one another. As I have loved you, so you must love one another. By this all men will know that you are my disciples, if you love one another"

John 13: 34 & 35

"I am the good shepherd; I know my sheep and my sheep know me -- just as the Father knows me and I know the Father -- and I lay down my life for the sheep. I have other sheep that are not of this sheep pen. I must bring them also. They too will listen to my voice and there shall be one flock and one shepherd."

John 10: 14-16

And, as the late Reverend Alexander Men, a modern-day Russian martyr, once wrote:

"Not doctrine or theory, but Christ Himself eternally renews Christianity and guides it into eternity." (4)

Within this book are three parts: Part I tells of the concept of preparing for the celebration of Christmas; Part II consists of daily readings for Advent; and Part III offers readings beginning on Christmas Eve and continuing through the Twelve Days of Christmas.

Because Eastern Christians observe this season as a forty day solemn fast, there are forty daily readings which, for them, begin on November 15. But because Western Christians begin Advent four Sundays before Christmas, the readings, for them, begin on that Sunday and the four Western Sundays are so noted in the text.

It is suggested that all begin at the beginning, and when the reader's own calendar reaches Christmas Eve, then go directly to Part III.

In this way, it doesn't matter whether one uses the Gregorian or Julian calendar, or whether the reader observes forty days or four weeks or any other particular period of time for Advent/Nativity Fast; the reader may use only what is useful and in whatever way desired.

For many, especially in the West, there will be extra days of readings. Westerners might wish to read twice a day for part of the time, or two readings on weekend days, or devise their own way of using all of the readings; or they might prefer to just skip over those that don't fit within their own time frame.

This is not in any way intended to take the place of church participation; it is only a small set of readings that one may do alone or with family or friends to hopefully enrich the spiritual side of the season. The readings are simple and, hopefully, uncontroversial, yet go to the core of what we as Christians all believe.

It is the writer's fervent wish and prayer that this little book will enable those of us of different traditions to pray together, seek His will together, and, in closeness, draw nearer to the Christ-Child, the Light of the world. May He brighten our pathway home to be with Him forever.

"Finally, all of you, live in harmony with one another; be sympathetic, love as brothers, be compassionate and humble."

1 Peter 3: 8

ADVENT (5)

"Come," Thou dost say to the Angels,
To the blessed spirits, "Come":
"Come," to the lambs of Thine own flock,
Thy little ones, "Come home."

"Come," from the many-mansioned house
The gracious word is sent;
"Come," from the ivory palaces
Unto the penitent.

O Lord, restore us deaf and blind,
Unclose our lips though dumb:
Then say to us, "I come with speed,"
And we will answer, "Come."

Christina Rossetti[2]

---

[2] Christina Rossetti, 19th century English poet and sister to poet Dante Rossetti, was a devout Anglican who expressed in her writings a deep love of God.

Part II

Chapter 3

FORTY DAILY READINGS FOR ADVENT

"Thou hast assumed a body of lowly clay, O Christ. ... By becoming mortal man yet remaining God, Thou hast raised us from death to life." (6)
               from Canon of Cosmas of Maiuma. Ode Three[3]

FIRST DAY IN ADVENT
FIRST SUNDAY IN WESTERN ADVENT

Isaiah 9: 6 & 7; John 3:16

Some seven hundred years *before* Christ's birth in Bethlehem, the Old Testament prophet Isaiah foretold:

"For to us a child is born,
to us a son given,
and the government will be on his shoulders.
And he will be called
Wonderful Counselor, Mighty God,
Everlasting Father, Prince of Peace.
Of the increase of his government and peace

---

[3] St. Cosmas and his brother St. Damien, were 4th century physicians known as "the moneyless ones" because they refused payment for their services to the poor. Devout Christians, they were martyred by beheading under Diocletian.

> *there will be no end.*
> *He will reign on David's throne*
> *and over his Kingdom,*
> *establishing and upholding it*
> *with justice and righteousness*
> *from that time on and forever.*
> *The zeal of the Lord Almighty*
> *will accomplish this."*
>
> Isaiah 9: 6 & 7

And shortly after Jesus left the earth, ascending to Heaven, His beloved disciple John wrote:

> "For God so loved the world that he gave his one and only Son, that whoever believes in him shall not perish but have eternal life."
>
> John 3:16

God-Gift; God-Child.

Struck by the magnitude of this, words fail, then come tumbling like an avalanche: God made man; Jesus -- a tiny Child in the miracle of divine birth; He gave us this because He loves us; Christ-Mass; Christmas; Advent; awesome anticipation. This -- the time of joyous waiting; the time of:

- Love.
- Hope.
- Joy.
- Peace.

The lamb of God made manifest among us!

O Lord, God almighty -- tender Child -- hear our prayer. You Who humbled Yourself to come in barest poverty, let us draw nearer to You this Advent season. Thank You for allowing us to think on the miracle of Your birth. Let us feel the warmth emanating from the light of Your manger-bed. If it be Your divine will, O blessed God-Baby, may we come closer to You this Advent season. Drawn by Your glorious sweetness from this guilt-ridden world, may we touch the hem of the fabric of the newness of Your life? As Your seasons unfold, from Advent/Nativity Fast and Christmas through Lent,

Easter/Pascha and the rest -- an eternally renewing circle -- surround us with the halo-light of Your love, and help us walk with You, sharing this ring of joy. Amen.

COME, THOU LONG EXPECTED JESUS (7)

Come, thou long-expected Jesus,
Born to set thy people free;
From our fears and sins release us,
Let is find our rest in Thee.

Israel's strength and consolation,
Hope of all the earth Thou art;
Dear desire of every nation,
Joy of every longing heart.

Born Thy people to deliver,
Born a Child and yet a King,
Born to reign in us forever,
Now Thy gracious kingdom bring.

By thine own eternal spirit
Rule in all our hearts alone:
By thine all-sufficing merit
Raise us to Thy glorious throne.

Charles Wesley 1744[4]

---

[4] An ordained Anglican minister, Charles Wesley was the brother of the John Wesley who founded Methodism in England. "Come, thou long-expected Jesus," first published in 1744, is one of eighteen poems he wrote about the birth of Jesus.

SECOND DAY IN ADVENT

Micah 5: 2, 4 & 5; Matthew 2:1, 4 - 6

The Old Testament prophet Micah predicted where Jesus would be born. He did this approximately seven hundred years before that miracle birth.

"But you, Bethlehem Ephrathah,
though you are small among the clans of Judah
out of you will come for me
one who will be ruler over Israel,
whose origins are from of old,
from ancient times."

Micah 5: 2

Matthew confirmed this when he wrote during the first century:

"After Jesus was born in Bethlehem in Judea, ..."

Matthew 2:1

"When he had called together all the people's chief priests and teachers of the law, he asked them where the Christ was to be born. 'In Bethlehem in Judea' they replied, 'for this is what the prophet has written:
'But you, Bethlehem, in the land of Judah,
are by no means least among the rulers of Judah;
for out of you will come a ruler
who will be the shepherd of my people Israel.'"

Matthew 2: 4 - 6

In considering the Old Testament prophecies pointing to the birth of Jesus, it is difficult to know where to begin, so many spoke of the different facets of His divine birth.

Micah, a contemporary of Isaiah, lived in Judah of which Bethlehem was a part. Although he plainly told that out of that little land the Christ would come, he lived hundreds of years before it happened. In Micah's writings, some of which were quoted to Herod at the time of Christ's birth, much is told about Jesus' life.

He described Jesus as the Shepherd feeding His flock:

"He will stand and shepherd his flock
in the strength of the Lord,
in the majesty of the name of the Lord his God.
And they will live securely,
for then his greatness will reach
to the ends of the earth."

Micah 5: 4

Micah also called Him a peacemaker, a deliverer, and a gatherer in of the remnant, and he spoke of Jesus' peace:

"And he will be their peace. ... ."

Micah 5: 5

O Lord, everlasting God, You Who have all power, yet Who came down to earth as the ultimate Gift, help us to renew the child-heart within us during this Advent time of reflection. Help us, Lord, to see You more clearly through a trusting child-like faith. Help us to humble ourselves and grow closer to You as we await the celebration of Your birthday. Amen.

THIRD DAY IN ADVENT

Isaiah 7:14; Matthew 1:18, 22 & 23; Luke 2:14; Isaiah 6: 3

Isaiah prophesied of Jesus' birth:

"Therefore the Lord himself will give you a sign: the virgin will be with child
and will give birth to a son, and will call him Immanuel."

Isaiah 7:14

Again, Matthew confirmed Isaiah's prophecies:

"This is how the birth of Jesus came about: His mother Mary was pledged to
be married to Joseph, but before they came together, she was found to be
with child through the holy spirit."

Matthew 1:18

Isaiah, who lived centuries before the divine birth, accurately described it. He called it a virgin birth and prophesied that *"a virgin will ... give birth to a son"* and even gave His name -- *"Immanuel."* Centuries later, not long after this prediction came to pass, Matthew repeated the story:

"All this took place to fulfill what the Lord had said through the prophet: 'The virgin will be with child and will give birth to a son, and they will call him 'Immanuel' -- which means, 'God with us'"

Matthew 1:22 & 23

When Isaiah was called by God to be a mighty prophet, he saw a vision of the Lord and His host of angels. Angels placed a live coal on his lips, purging him. Then the angels sang praises to God.

*"Holy, holy, holy is the Lord Almighty;
the whole earth is full of his glory."*

Isaiah 6:3

Again, angels sang when Jesus was born fulfilling Isaiah's prophecy:

*"Glory to God in the highest,
and on earth peace ... ."*

Luke 2:14

Lord Jesus, gentle Child, guide our feet, strengthen the depth of our repentence, and purge our sins. Grant us the grace to overcome them so that with clean lips we may sing Your praises now and always. Humble us, Lord; let us kneel to the level of little children, realizing that all we are or ever shall be is only an infinitesimally small part of Your Christmas Love-Gift to us, sinners who love You. Amen.

THE STORY OF ZECHARIAH

As Told by Saint Luke

"In the time of Herod king of Judea there was a priest named Zechariah who belonged to the priestly division of Abijah; his wife Elizabeth was also a descendant of Aaron. Both of them were upright in the sight of God,

observing all the Lord's commandments and regulations blamelessly. But they had no children, because Elizabeth was barren; and they were both well along in years.

Once when Zechariah's division was on duty and he was serving as priest before God, he was chosen by lot, according to the custom of the priesthood, to go into the temple of the Lord and burn incense. And when the time for the burning of incense came, all the assembled worshipers were praying outside. Then an angel of the Lord appeared to him, standing at the right side of the altar of incense. When Zechariah saw him, he was startled and gripped with fear. But the angel said to him: 'Do not be afraid, Zechariah; your prayer has been heard. Your wife Elizabeth will bear you a son, and you are to give him the name John. He will be a joy and delight to you, and many will rejoice because of his birth, for he will be great in the sight of the Lord. He is never to take wine or other fermented drink, and will be filled with the Holy Spirit even from birth. Many of the people of Israel will he bring back to the Lord their God. And he will go on before the Lord in the spirit and power of Elijah, to turn the hearts of the fathers to their children and the disobedient to the wisdom of the righteous -- to make ready a people prepared for the Lord.'

Zechariah asked the angel. 'How can I be sure of this? I am an old man and my wife is well on in years.'

The angel answered, 'I am Gabriel. I stand in the presence of God, and I have been sent to speak to you and to tell you this good news. And now you will be silent and not able to speak until the day this happens, because you did not believe my words, which will come true at their proper time.'

Meanwhile, the people were waiting for Zechariah and wondering why he stayed so long in the temple. When he came out, he could not speak to them. They realized he had seen a vision in the temple, for he kept making signs to them but remained unable to speak.

When his time of service was completed, he returned home. After this his wife Elizabeth became pregnant and for five months remained in seclusion. 'The Lord has done this for me,' she said. 'In these days he has shown his favor and taken away my disgrace among the people.'"

Luke 1: 5 – 25

FOURTH DAY IN ADVENT

Luke 1: 13 & 15 & 16

Before Jesus was born, God prepared the way by sending John. Before John was born, God prepared the way by creating a life-long hunger for a child in the elderly and barren Elizabeth and her husband Zechariah. And before Elizabeth conceived, God prepared Zechariah. These things He did in preparation for the "Advent" of Jesus' birth in Bethlehem.

"Do not be afraid, Zechariah; your prayer has been heard."

Luke 1: 13

"... he will be filled with the Holy Spirit even from birth. Many of the people of Israel will he bring back to the Lord their God."

Luke 1:15 & 16

Miracles surround Jesus' birth and life, but one of the first was that of Zechariah. When this good old gentleman priest was told the wonderful news that his elderly wife Elizabeth would conceive and bear him a son who would *" ... be filled with the Holy Spirit ... ,"* Zechariah questioned the angel asking how this could be because of their ages. Then the angel identified himself. *"I am Gabriel. I stand in the presence of God, ..."* and Zechariah was struck dumb because of his doubt until after his son John was born.

Zechariah was told that his son would be great in the sight of the Lord, and would go before Him filled with the Holy Spirit, and would prepare the way for Him. What joy for Zechariah and Elizabeth who never gave up in their prayers and faith, to be so blessed and used as instruments for God's holy will!

O Lord, prepare our hearts and souls during this Advent season for the celebration of the coming of your beloved Son. Forgive and cleanse us, Father-Son-and-Holy Spirit, from sin that we may be washed clean. May we, by Your grace, be ever faithful and true as were Elizabeth and Zechariah. Thank You Heavenly Father, for Your divine Son. Amen.

FIFTH DAY IN ADVENT

Luke 1: 68-79.

Zechariah's Benedictus

On the eighth day after the miraculous birth of John, the family and friends of Zechariah and Elizabeth gathered to share their joy. It was the time of the infant's circumcision and naming. Everyone expected the baby to be called after his father, but the angel Gabriel had told Zechariah what to name this miracle child of their old age.

Zechariah, who had not been able to speak since he first doubted the miracle-birth, wrote on a tablet, *"John."* Then his tongue was loosed, and he was filled with the Holy Spirit and he began speaking these beautiful words:

"Praise be to the Lord, the God of Israel,
because he has come and has redeemed his people.
He has raised up a horn of salvation for us
in the house of his servant David
(as he said through his holy prophets of long ago),
salvation from our enemies
and from the hand of all who hate us --
to show mercy to our fathers
and to remember his holy covenant,
the oath he swore to our father Abraham:
to rescue us from the hand of our enemies,
and to enable us to serve him without fear
in holiness and righteousness before him all our days.
And you, my child, will be called
a prophet of the Most High
for you will go before the Lord to prepare a way for him,
to give his people the knowledge of salvation
through the forgiveness of their sins,
because of the tender mercy of our God,
by which the rising sun will come to us from heaven
to shine on those living in darkness
and in the shadow of death,
to guide our feet into the path of peace."

Luke 1: 68 - 79

All the people gathered there that day marveled and treasured this in their hearts, wondering at the prophecies of Zechariah and the miracle they beheld.

Holy Lord, we too have heard the prophecies and been blessed to hear the miraculous wonder of Your words. You, to Whom nothing is impossible, surround us with Your peace this holy season; crowd out the clamor of the world and guide our feet in Your way of compassion and love. Amen.

SIXTH DAY IN ADVENT

Luke 1: 26 - 38; Isaiah 7:14

The Annunciation

There had long been a darkness on the earth. The Old Testament is filled with the voice of a people oppressed, seeking their way out of the gloom of the world and worldliness. The Psalms lift up a plaintiff voice, as if the very soul of mankind crying out, seeking the goodness, wisdom and light of God -- beseeching a closer walk with the almighty Creator of the Universe. There came a time almost devoid of hope and goodness, although throughout history many had prophesied a Messiah. The wait had been long; the need great.

Reverend Alexander Men described this time in history.

> *"The hope that the one who would lead the world out of this labyrinth would appear was revived from time to time. The poet Vergil foretold the birth of a young boy from which the age of Saturn would begin. The Buddhists waited for Maitreya Buddha, the Hindus the next incarnation of the god Vishnu, the Persians the Savior-Saoshiant, the Jews the Messiah... . In Palestine, the atmosphere of mystical aspirations thickened with each passing year. Finally ... ." (8)*

Yes, finally, near the time the angel Gabriel visited Zechariah to announce the forthcoming birth of John the Baptist, God sent Gabriel to Mary. Imagine Mary's wonder at his announcement. The angel assured her by his simple statement that *"nothing is impossible to God."* Here is that blessed encounter:

"In the sixth month, God sent the angel Gabriel to Nazareth, a town in Galilee, to a virgin pledged to be married to a man named Joseph, a descendent of David. The virgin's name was Mary. The angel went to her and said, 'Greetings, you who are highly favored! The Lord is with you.' Mary was greatly troubled at his words and wondered what kind of greeting this might be. But the angel said to her, 'Do not be afraid, Mary, you have found favor with God. You will be with child and give birth to a son, and you are to give him the name Jesus. He will be great and will be called the Son of the Most High. The Lord God will give him the throne of his father David, and he will reign over the house of Jacob forever; his kingdom will never end.' 'How can this be,' Mary asked the angel, 'since I am a virgin?' The angel answered, 'The Holy Spirit will come upon you, and the power of the Most High will overshadow you. So the holy one to be born will be called the Son of God. Even Elizabeth your relative is going to have a child in her old age, and she who was said to be barren is in her sixth month. For nothing is impossible with God.' 'I am the Lord's servant,' Mary answered. 'May it be to me as you have said.'"

Luke 1: 26-38

These astonishing words again echoed Isaiah's prophesy hundreds of years earlier foretelling that:

"Therefore the Lord himself will give you a sign: The virgin will be with child and will give birth to a son, and will call him Immanuel."

Isaiah 7:14

Both angels and prophets were very active in announcements surrounding the birth of Jesus, intertwining wondrous words between the Old and the New Testaments. From centuries past down through the annals of time, all voiced the same story; they told of the divine and miraculous birth -- God's Son, born of a virgin, come to earth. Immanuel -- God-with-us.

Holy Child of God -- Immanuel -- hear our prayer. Let the magnificence of Your coming to earth be always imprinted in our awareness, lest we forget and become lost in the tinsel of this world. Now that You have come, bringing Light and goodness to this place of darkness and evil, O divine One, grant us a spark of intelligence to understand, in our finite way, something of the depth of meaning of this holy Advent-Christmas season, surrounding us with Your Love. Amen.

SEVENTH DAY IN ADVENT

Luke 1: 39-45

The Visitation

The angel Gabriel foretold that even from the womb, Elizabeth's son John would be filled with the Holy Spirit, and when Mary went to visit Elizabeth, the unborn John leapt in his mother's womb for joy. When this happened, John's mother Elizabeth was filled with the Holy Spirit and *knew* that Mary was with child and that that Child was the Lord.

> *"At that time Mary got ready and hurried to a town in the hill country of Judea where she entered Zechariah's home and greeted Elizabeth. When Elizabeth heard Mary's greeting, the baby leapt in her womb, and Elizabeth was filled with the Holy Spirit. In a loud voice she exclaimed: 'Blessed are you among women, and blessed is the child you will bear! But why am I so favored, that the mother of my Lord should come to me? As soon as the sound of your greeting reached my ears, the baby in my womb leapt for joy. Blessed is she who has believed that what the Lord has said to her will be accomplished!'"*
>
> Luke 1: 39-45

It must have been great comfort for Mary, the young cousin of elderly Elizabeth, to be in the presence of another person who was expecting a miraculous birth although in a lesser way, yet one who understood the full portent -- the full meaning -- and shared the joy. Also, to Elizabeth who was in her sixth month of pregnancy, what comfort it must have been to have Mary come and share time with her during the last months before giving birth in her old age. While few in the world knew or understood, these two blessed women could share and encourage one another.

Elizabeth must have thought of Sarah who, centuries earlier and also in her old age, was visited by an angel who foretold her giving birth to a son, Isaac, when her husband was one hundred years old. As Matthew tells in the first chapter of his book, Jesus is the direct descendent through his adoptive father Joseph from that miraculous birth. From Abraham to David were fourteen generations; from David to the Babylonian deportation were fourteen generations; from then until Christ's birth were fourteen generations -- three perfect sets of fourteen.

O Lord, You Who revealed Yourself through many miracles and mysteries from the beginnings of time, allow us never even for a moment to forget the preciousness of Your magnificent, incomprehensible and most miraculous Gift -- the infant Jesus, God-on-Earth. May we, so blessed, open our hearts to share this wondrous Love with one another as You told us to do. In Jesus' holy Name we ask. Amen.

EIGHTH DAY IN ADVENT
SECOND SUNDAY IN WESTERN ADVENT

Luke 1: 46-55; Isaiah 61: 10 & 11

The Magnificat

One of the most repeated and beloved biblical passages is known as The Magnificat -- Mary's answer to Elizabeth.

"And Mary said:
'My soul glorifies the Lord
and my spirit rejoices in God my savior.
for he has been mindful
of the humble state of his servant.
From now on all generations will call me blessed,
for the Mighty One has done great things for me --
holy is his name.
His mercy extends to those who fear him,
from generation to generation.
He has performed mighty deeds with his arm;
he has scattered those who are proud
in their inmost thoughts.
He has brought down rulers from their thrones
but has lifted up the humble.
He has filled the hungry with good things
but has sent the rich away empty.
He has helped his servant Israel,

remembering to be merciful
to Abraham and his descendants forever,
even as he said to our fathers.'"

Luke 1: 46 - 55

Here, Mary responds to Elizabeth's inspired greeting when the infant John leapt for joy in her womb because he was in the presence of his Lord by the nearness of Mary and her unborn Child. In this, Mary sings praises and proclaims the greatness of God. Consider it in comparison to Isaiah's prophecy made thousands of years earlier:

"I delight greatly in the Lord;
my soul rejoices in my God.
For he has clothed me with garments of salvation
and arrayed me in a robe of righteousness...
so the sovereign Lord will make
righteousness and praise spring up before all nations."

Isaiah 61:10 & 11

Today, at the place called Ein Karem (Vineyard Spring) in the Holy Lands, on the hill where it is believed Mary met Elizabeth while they were both with child, this Magnificat is inscribed on dozens of plaques, each in a different language.

Mary's response echoes many of the Psalms and seems to foreshadow Stephen's sermon in Acts 7. In utmost humility (His lowly handmaiden), the chosen Mary exalts her God, offers her willingness, and proclaims the importance of the forthcoming birth of Christ.

Lord God, heavenly Father, You Who gave Your divine Son to be born in humility that we may live, have mercy us, forgive our sins, and renew a right spirit within us. May our souls and lives glorify You, and our spirits rejoice in You, always. Amen.

NINTH DAY IN ADVENT

1 Samuel 2: 1-10; Jeremiah 31: 15

The Song of Hannah

Hannah's song, sung over a thousand years before the birth of Jesus, seems also a presager to that of Mary's Magnificat. It, too, came from a woman who yielded to God's will (though of course in a much lesser way) -- one who gave a son back to God -- and it is strangely prophetic. When God allowed this barren woman to bear a son, she sang this song of thanksgiving:

> "My heart rejoices in the Lord;
> in the Lord my horn is lifted high.
> My mouth boasts over my enemies,
> for I delight in your deliverance.
> There is no one holy like the Lord;
> there is no one besides you;
> there is no rock like our God.
> Do not keep talking so proudly
> or let your mouth speak such arrogance
> for the Lord is a God who knows,
> and by him deeds are weighed.
> The bows of the warriors are broken,
> but those who stumble are armed with strength.
> Those who were full hire themselves out for food,
> but those who were hungry hunger no more.
> She who was barren has born seven children,
> but she who has had many sons pines away.
> The Lord brings death and makes alive;
> he brings down to the grave and raises up.
> The Lord sends poverty and wealth;
> he humbles and he exhalts.
> He raises the poor from the dust
> and lifts the needy from the ash heap;
> he seats them with princes
> and has them inherit a throne of honor.
> For the foundations of the earth are the Lord's;
> upon them he has set the world.

He will guard the feet of his saints,
but the wicked will be silenced in darkness.
It is not by strength that one prevails;
those who oppose the Lord will be shattered
He will thunder against them from heaven;
the Lord will judge the ends of the earth."

1 Samuel 2: 1-10

Hannah came from Ramah where it seems that one of the Rachels of the Bible lived, the Rachel who wept for her children slain by Herod's soldiers in their quest to kill the Christ-Child. This, too, was prophesied in olden times by the prophet Jeremiah when he said:

"A voice is heard in Ramah, mourning and great weeping, Rachel weeping for her children and refusing to be comforted, because her children are no more."

Jeremiah 31: 15

This prophesy came some six hundred years before the birth of Jesus, and over four hundred years after the time of Hannah -- criss-crossing and interweaving Biblical history with prophesy concerning miraculous birth, maternal love, first born sons, divine intercession, and the anguish and joy of motherhood.

Another Rachel who wept for her children who were not, was the Rachel of the Old Testament. This Rachel, Jacob's wife, waited, weeping, many years before being able to bear her virtuous son, Joseph.

Hannah prayed for a child and was blessed with a son whom she returned to God as soon as he was weaned from the breast. This son became the beloved prophet and judge, Samuel.

Lord, help us to yield ourselves to You. Although we can never fully understand the mystery and meaning of what happens in our lives, let us accept -- as did the Rachels, Hannah, Elizabeth and Mary -- whatever comes, holding fast to what You would have us to do according to Your Commandments. Blend our lives into the harmony of the wondrous fabric of Your holy will. Amen.

TENTH DAY IN ADVENT

Isaiah 7: 14; Matthew 1: 18-23; Psalm 130: 8

Matthew tells simply of how Jesus came to earth:

"This is how the birth of Jesus Christ came about: His mother Mary was pledged to be married to Joseph, but before they came together, she was found to be with child through the Holy Spirit. Because Joseph her husband was a righteous man and did not want to expose her to public disgrace, he had in mind to divorce her quietly. But after he had considered this, an angel of the Lord appeared to him in a dream and said, 'Joseph son of David, do not be afraid to take Mary home as your wife, because what is conceived in her is from the Holy Spirit. She will give birth to a son and you are to give him the name Jesus, because he will save his people from their sins. All this took place to fulfill what the Lord had said through the prophet: 'The virgin will be with child and will give birth to a son, and they will call him Immanuel.' -- which means, 'God is with us.'"

Matthew 1: 18-23

Here again, Isaiah's words, centuries earlier, were repeated:

"Therefore the Lord himself will give you a sign: The virgin will be with child and will give birth to a son, and will call him Immanuel."

Isaiah 7:14

Joseph, betrothed to the young virgin Mary, was naturally troubled to learn she was with child, but unlike Zechariah who was struck dumb for his doubts, Joseph listened well to the angel who appeared to him in a dream. Joseph both listened *and* obeyed. He was told that Mary would bear a Son who "*... will save the people from their sins.*" This was as the Psalmist prophesied many years before:

"He himself will redeem Israel from all their sins."

Psalm 130: 8

Again, an angel of God intervenes in the circumstances of Jesus' birth. Again, a reference back through hundreds of years to the prophets' foretelling of Mary's miraculous birth of one to be called "Immanuel."

How many times and how many ways You speak to us, Lord -- through the prophets -- through the angels -- through Your written Word? How the intermingling weaves a perfect and mysterious fabric! O Lord, Immanuel, thank You for coming to earth. Thank You for being God-with-us. Keep us close beside You always. Help us never to stray, but when we do become lost, pick us up and set us back on the path that leads to You. Amen.

VENI EMMANUEL (9)

O come, O come Emmanuel,
And ransom captive Israel,
That mourns in lonely exile here
Until the Son of God appear.
Rejoice! Rejoice! Emmanuel
Shall come to thee, O Israel!

O come, thou wisdom from on high,
Who orderest all things mightily;
To us the path of knowledge show,
And teach us in her ways to go.
Rejoice! Rejoice! Emmanuel
Shall come to thee, O Israel!

O come, O come, thou Lord of might,
Who to thy tribes on Sinai's height
In ancient times didst give the law,
In cloud, and majesty, and awe.
Rejoice! Rejoice! Emmanuel
Shall come to thee, O Israel!

O come, thou rod of Jesse's stem,
From every foe deliver them
That trust thy mighty power to save,
And give them victory o'er the grave.
Rejoice! Rejoice! Emmanuel
Shall come to thee, O Israel!

> O come, thou key of David, come,
> And open wide our heavenly home;
> Make safe the way that leads on high,
> And close the door to misery.
> Rejoice! Rejoice! Emmanuel
> Shall come to thee, O Israel!
>
> O come, thou Dayspring from on high,
> And cheer us by thy drawing nigh;
> Disperse the gloomy clouds of night,
> And death's dark shadow put to flight.
> Rejoice! Rejoice! Emmanuel
> Shall come to thee, O Israel!
>
> O come, desire of nations, bind
> In one the hearts of all mankind;
> Bid thou our sad divisions cease,
> And be thyself our King of Peace.
> Rejoice! Rejoice! Emmanuel
> Shall come to thee, O Israel!
>
> Latin 9th century[5]

ELEVENTH DAY IN ADVENT

John 1: 1-5, 8: 58; Micah 5:2; Psalm 102: 25 - 27

It is good during this Advent season to remind ourselves that Jesus was from the beginning of time with the Father -- that He always was and always will be. He was and is the Light and through Him, all that is good came to be.

"In the beginning was the Word:

---

[5] This ancient carol, written in Latin by an anonymous author possibly as early as the ninth century, was known as "The Great O's" as each verse told of one of the attributes of Jesus. One of these verses was chanted each day, along with the Magnificat, in the liturgy in the medieval church on the seven days just prior to Christmas. In 1851, an English language version by John Mason Neale was published in England.

and the Word was with God
and the Word was God.
He was with God in the beginning.
Through him all things were made;
without him nothing was made that has been made.
In him was life,
and that life was the light of men.
The light shines in the darkness,
but the darkness has not understood."

John 1: 1-5

Jesus Himself said:

"'I tell you the truth,' Jesus answered, 'before Abraham was born, I am.'"

John 8: 58

Again, Micah, some seven hundred years before Christ came to earth, when he was predicting the birth of Jesus in Bethlehem, mentioned His origins:

"But you, Bethlehem Ephratha,
though you are small among the clans of Judah,
out of you will come for me
one who will be ruler over Israel,
whose origins are from of old,
from ancient times."

Micah 5: 2

The Psalmist adds:

"In the beginning you laid the foundations of the earth,
and the heavens are the work of your hands.
They will perish, but you remain;
they will all wear out like a garment.
Like clothing you will change them
and they will be discarded.
But you remain the same,
and your years will never end."

Psalm 102: 25-27

Lord, You Who humbled Yourself to come as a little Child to live in our sinful world and give it Light -- You Who have all power and Who always was and always will be, forevermore, forgive and have mercy on us, Your children. Help us to humble ourselves and follow You; enable us to share Your glorious Light within the darkness on the earth. You, Whose *"life was the light of men,"* have mercy on us and hear our prayer. Amen.

TWELFTH DAY IN ADVENT

John 10: 30; 17: 5 & 24; Genesis 1: 26

In the first chapter of Genesis, at the time of the creation, God spoke of "us" and "our."
He said:

"Let us make man in our image, in our likeness, ..."

Genesis 1: 26

Thousands of years later, John wrote in quoting Jesus:

"Father,
I want those you have given me
to be with me where I am, and to see my glory,
the glory you have given me
because you loved me before the creation of the world."

John 17: 24

That Jesus existed long before He came down that first Christmas as Love incarnate has been attested to many times. Here, in Jesus' prayer to God the Father, He affirmed that He was *"before the creation of the world."*
Earlier in that same prayer, He said:

"And now, Father, glorify me in your presence with the glory I had with you before the world began."

John 17: 5.

John again quoted Jesus as saying:

"I and the Father are one."

John 10: 30

O God the Father, God the Son, and God the Holy Spirit, You who came down as a tiny Child that first Christmas day two thousand years ago, showering us with love -- love us still. Forgive our sins that we might be cleansed and receive the enfolding of Your graciousness. Help us as we wander this world seeking our way home to You Who always was and always will be. Guide our feet, light our pathway, and give us strength, wisdom and grace to be true to You, now and forevermore. Amen.

THIRTEENTH DAY IN ADVENT

Genesis 22: 18; Acts 3: 25; Hebrews 11: 9 & 10

Jesus has been called "The Promised seed of Abraham" -- the fulfillment of the prophecy made two thousand years before His divine birth.

Abraham was visited by angels who told him he and his barren wife Sarah would have a son in their old age. Many consider that these three angels were the Holy Trinity.

At that time, God also told Abraham that his descendants would become great and that all the nations of the earth would be blessed by him. Geneologically, Jesus is a descendant of Abraham through his adoptive father, Joseph. It is said that Jesus was the principal fulfillment of that promise.

Later, Abraham was tested by God, being told to sacrifice his beloved son Isaac, the one given in Abraham's old age. This seems symbolically a shadow of the supreme sacrifice of Jesus, the Lamb of God, God the Father's own beloved Son. At this time, God told Abraham again that *"... and through your offspring all the nations of the earth will be blessed ... .."* (Genesis 22: 18).

Jesus Himself, some two thousand years later, said:

"Your father Abraham rejoiced at the thought of seeing my day; he saw it and was glad."

John 8: 56

Peter also told of this when he quoted the Lord as saying to Abraham:

"Through your offspring, all peoples on earth will be blessed."
Acts 3: 25

In the book of Hebrews, this is again spoken of when telling about Abraham:

"By faith he made his home in the promised land like a stranger in a foreign country; he lived in tents, as did Isaac and Jacob, who were heirs with him of the same promise. For he was looking forward to the city with foundations, whose architect and builder is God."
Hebrews 11: 9 & 10

O Lord Jesus, Son of Abraham -- Son of God yet very God -- look down on us, Your children. Grant us the unswerving faithfulness of Abraham. Forgive our sin and let us walk with You, surrounded always by Your love. Amen.

FOURTEENTH DAY IN ADVENT

Genesis 17: 19; 26: 24; Matthew 1: 2; Luke 3: 34

Jesus has been called the *"Promised seed of Isaac."* God told Abraham that *"... your wife Sarah will bear you a son and you will call him Isaac. I will establish my covenant with him as an everlasting covenant for his descendants after him."*
Genesis 17: 19

Isaac, the long awaited son of Abraham and Sarah, had many desirable qualities. He even submitted obediently as his father Abraham prepared to offer him as a living sacrifice. (Genesis 22: 6 -9)

Isaac was a meditator and an affectionate person, loving his parents and his wife Rebecca. (Genesis 24) He was peaceful and prayerful. A story is told of how peaceful this man was. As his servants dug wells of spring water, if any shepherds claimed them, he did not argue but moved on until there was no dispute. (Genesis 26: 19-23)

In Beersheba, God told Isaac:

"I am the God of your father Abraham.
Do not be afraid, for I am with you.
I will bless you and increase the number
of your descendants for the sake of my servant Abraham."

Genesis 26: 24

In the New Testament, both Matthew and Luke, in their genealogical listings, spoke of Jesus as being the descendent of Isaac.

O Lord God, You Who centuries ago established a covenant blessing those who love and obey You, help us to establish within ourselves the qualities of Isaac -- meditation, affection, peaceableness and prayerfulness. May we walk honorably in the world, so as to set a fine example as Isaac did. Thank You, Lord, for Your bountiful blessings culminating in the incomprehensible -- Your divine Gift of Your beloved Son, Jesus. Amen.

LITTLE JESUS (10)

Little baby
come to be
living here
on earth -- like me.
You --
the Son of God on high,
in
a little manger lie.

Little God-Child
will You be
ever close
and near to me?
You --
come down from heaven above
just
to share Your great-sweet love.

Little Gift
from heaven above --

little Jesus,
made of Love.
You --
the Son of God on high,
in
a little manger lie.

Little Jesus,
from above --
little Jesus --
You I love.
You --
the son of God on high --
come
to earth to live and die.

FIFTEENTH DAY IN ADVENT
THIRD SUNDAY IN WESTERN ADVENT

Gaudette (Joyful) Sunday

Psalm 30: 5; Luke 2: 9 - 12; John 15:11;16: 24

The seasons of Advent and of Christmas are filled with the most unsurpassable joy! Yes, there is great joy and wonder associated with all of the seasons of the church year, but this one comes with hardly a hint of pain or sorrow. It is a most pure and unmitigated happiness, the coming to the earth of Jesus.

> ".... weeping may remain for a night, but rejoicing comes in the morning."
> Psalm 30: 5

From the beginnings of time there had been a kind of darkness. There was a separation from God the Father; there was a not-fully-knowing of Him -- a lack of understanding. The world and its people knew God but in a limited way. He was a mighty, all-powerful Creator, One to be feared and loved, but there was not yet the revelation of His inestimable compassion revealed in Jesus Who taught the tempering of The Law with love. There is such peace in knowing Him, visualizing Him on earth, hearing the wonder of His spoken Word in parables, feeling His compassion -- His tender mercies; and then there was His ultimate Gift in His mission that we *"might have life and have it more abundantly."*

There is an old adage that it is always darkest before the dawn, and Jesus brought that dawn; so there was, after the long night, the *"rejoicing"* that *"comes in the morning."*

The angels told "good *news of great joy"* when they appeared to the shepherds.

> *"An angel of the Lord appeared to them, and the glory of the Lord shone around them, and they were terrified. But the angel said to them, 'Do not be afraid. I bring you good news of great joy that will be for all the people. Today in the town of David a Savior has been born to you; he is Christ the Lord. This will be a sign to you: You will find a baby wrapped in clothes and lying in a manger.'"*
>
> Luke 2: 9-12

When Jesus told His disciples that they must keep His Commandments, He associated this with joy. Not as a hardship in the Pharisaical way. He said:

> *"I have told you this*
> *so that my joy may be in you*
> *and that your joy may be complete."*
>
> John 15:11

Here He actually gave us a way to experience His own joy.

And, when John told of Jesus' giving one of His bountiful, gracious and almost-unbelievable gifts, He said that Jesus did this so *"that your joy may be complete"*:

> *"Until now you have not asked for anything in my name.*
> *Ask and you will receive,*
> *and your joy will be complete."*
>
> John 16: 24

Throughout the year, when hardships come, when times are difficult and it is hard to smile, I think on Christmas, and am renewed. It is then that I pray to God and feel an incredibly indescribable warmth, as if bathed in a downpouring of heavenly love.

Dear Lord Jesus, thank You for the wondrous joy in Your coming to the confusion and darkness of earth, offering us Your Light and directing us toward all that is good, pure and noble. Bless those who suffer and have difficulty feeling joy for whatever reason; relieve their pain and let them rejoice in Your bountiful love and tender mercies. Help us to help them. We ask in Jesus' holy Name. Amen.

SIXTEENTH DAY IN ADVENT

Matthew 1: 2 -16; Numbers 24:17
Genesis 28: 14; 49:10; Psalm 46: 1, 2 & 7

Jesus is called "The Promised Seed of Jacob."

"Abraham was the father of Isaac, Isaac the father of Jacob, Jacob the father of ... [many generations mentioned here] ... and Jacob [another Jacob] the father of Joseph, the husband of Mary, of whom was born Jesus, who is called Christ."

Matthew 1: 2 -16

Jacob, the grandson of Abraham by Isaac, was much blessed by God. He was given a vision of a ladder leading to heaven when he was promised that God would be with him and multiply his descendants to a mighty nation. The place where this happened he called *Bethel*. God then renamed Jacob "Israel" and from this nation of Israel came our Lord through Mary in Bethlehem. Prophecies of the Messiah are made concerning Jacob:

"A star will come out of Jacob; a scepter will rise ... ."

Numbers 24: 17

And again:

"Your descendants will be like the dust of the earth, and you will spread out to the west and the east, to the north and to the south. All peoples on earth will be blessed through you... ."

Genesis 28: 14

The Psalmist spoke of *"the God of Jacob"* in this magnificent and comforting passage:

*"God is our refuge and strength,
an ever-present help in trouble.
Therefore we will not fear,
though the earth give way
and the mountains fall into the heart of the sea, ...
The Lord Almighty is with us;
the God of Jacob is our fortress."*

Psalm 46: 1, 2 & 7

When Jacob was old and giving his final blessing to his children, he prophesied the Messiah:

*"The scepter will not depart from Judah,
nor the ruler's staff from between his feet,
until he comes to whom it belongs
and the obedience of the nations is his."*

Genesis 49: 10

Dear Jesus, the promised Messiah, help us render obedience to You regardless of the pressures, clamor and distractions of the world. You Who are the promised Star of Jacob, grant us the grace to follow Your Light, always remembering its radiance over the stable at Bethlehem. Amen.

SEVENTEENTH DAY IN ADVENT

Matthew 3: 1; Isaiah 40: 3; Mark 1: 2 - 4, 7 & 8

The forerunner of Jesus' coming, John the Baptist, warned people repeatedly to:

Advent Anticipation: Drawing Nearer to the Christ-Child

"Repent, for the kingdom of heaven is near."

Matthew 3: 1

Centuries before the time of John, the Prophet Isaiah spoke of him:

"A voice of one calling: 'In the desert prepare the way of the Lord; ... .'"

Isaiah 40: 3

In this Advent season -- the time of preparing ourselves for the symbolic coming again of Christ at Christmas, we need to do as John said. We need to "make his paths straight." Just as a householder in Jesus' day "killed the fatted calf" in preparing a feast for a fine visitor or the return of family; and just as a house is swept clean today in preparation for visitors, how much more should we prepare ourselves for His coming?

What a wonderful time -- this awesome anticipation of the joyful celebration of Love-Made-Manifest when God blesses the world with a blanket of warmth of sharing and caring -- is this time of seeking to cleanse ourselves inwardly before Christmas.

As John said -- *"Repent!"*

Mark, in Isaiah, quotes God's words about John:

"It is written in Isaiah the prophet:
'I will send my messenger ahead of you,
who will prepare your way --
a voice of one calling in the desert,
'Prepare the way for the Lord,
make straight paths for him.'"

Mark 1: 2 & 3

Then Mark tells how John, *"... came, baptizing in the desert region and preaching a baptism of repentance for the forgiveness of sins."* Mark 1: 4

Throngs of people of Judaea, the little land where Jesus was born, came to John and confessed their sins, repenting. This Judaea, surprisingly, is today much as it was then -- a place often hot and arid, yet also a place of gently rolling hills laced with grape vines and olive trees. Paths lead up and down the softly sloping hills. Mary climbed them when she went to visit Elizabeth. When John told the people to *"make straight the way,"* one can imagine the symbolism in their minds of straightening out the undulating land on which they lived. But straightening out our souls, making them clean and smooth, is an equally formidable task.

John spoke of the One for whom we should prepare when he said:

"After me will come one more powerful than I, the thongs of whose sandals I am not worthy to stoop down and untie. I baptize you with water, but he will baptize you with the Holy Spirit."

Mark 1: 7 & 8

Lord God, heavenly Father -- You Who gave the world your only begotten Son -- help us to truly, deeply and thoroughly repent of our sins that we may, with clean hearts and renewed spirits, draw closer to You this holy season. May we be heartily sorry for having offended You in any way -- by thought, word, or deed -- by our sins of omission as well as of commission. Help us to lead purer lives so that we may, in our own small part of the universe, make the path straighter before You. Amen.

GOD BE IN MY HEAD (11)

God be in my head, and in my understanding;
God be in my eyes, and in my looking;
God be in my mouth, and in my speaking;
God be in my heart, and in my thinking;
God be at mine end, and at my departing.

Sarum Printer, 1558[6]

EIGHTEENTH DAY IN ADVENT

Isaiah 40: 3-5; Luke 3: 4 - 6, 17

Isaiah, who lived over seven hundred years before John the Baptist, described him and his message well:
"A voice of one calling:

---

[6] These words are from the Sarum Primer, a collection of hymns in the style known as Sarum (Salisbury) that originated in the Salisbury Cathedral in the city of the same name in England.

Advent Anticipation: Drawing Nearer to the Christ-Child

'In the desert prepare the way for the Lord;
make straight in the wilderness a highway for our God
Every valley shall be raised up,
every mountain and hill made low;
the rough ground shall become level,
the rugged places a plain.'"

Isaiah 40: 3-5

Luke, a contemporary of John the Baptist, echoed these words of Isaiah in his own description made some seven hundred years later.

"A voice of one calling in the desert,
'Prepare the way for the Lord,
make straight paths for him.
Every valley shall be filled in,
every mountain and hill made low.
The crooked roads shall become straight,
the rough ways smooth.
And all mankind will see God's salvation.'"

Luke 3: 4 - 6

When the people heard these words from John, they asked what they must do. John told them that a person with two coats should share one and that people with food should also share. Money collectors were told to take no more than was just. They were told not to intimidate, nor extort, and to be content with their pay.

John repeatedly exhorted the people simply to "Repent" -- to be truly sorry for all their wrongdoings.

He described Jesus as one with a winnowing fan -- that instrument farmers in those days used to separate the wheat from the weeds -- the chaff. John described Jesus as separating the good people from the bad -- the "chaff," and that "...*he will burn up the chaff with unquenchable fire."* (Luke 3: 17)

O Lord, have mercy on us, forgive our manifold sin and hear our prayer. Help us to be just, but tempered with love; help us to be kind and compassionate in our dealings with others. Help us to share what You have given to us by helping the poor and pained -- the weak and lost. May we know the joy that comes in doing Your will. May we and our loved ones be within the wheat in your winnowing fan. Amen.

ON JORDAN'S BANK (12)

On Jordan's bank the Baptist's cry
Announces that the Lord is nigh;
Awake and hearken, for he brings
Glad tidings of the King of Kings.

Then cleansed be every beast from sin;
Make straight the way of God within,
And let each heart prepare a home
Where such a mighty guest may come.

For Thou art our salvation, Lord,
Our refuge, and our great reward;
Without Thy grace we waste away
Like flowers that wither and decay.

To heal the sick, stretch out Thy hand,
And bid the fallen sinner stand;
Shine forth and let Thy grace restore
Earth's own true loveliness once more.

All praise, eternal Son, to thee,
Whose advent doth thy people free;
Whom with the Father we adore
And Holy Ghost for evermore. Amen.

Charles Coffin[7]

---

[7] Originally written in Latin by Charles Coffin, author of over a hundred hymns and Rector of the College of Beauvais at the University of Paris, these verses were first published in 1736 in a collection of his works entitled *Paris Breviary*. In 1837, two of the verses were translated into English by John Chandler; the translator of the other verses is unknown.

NINETEENTH DAY IN ADVENT

John 1: 6-8; 15-17

The beloved apostle John described John the Baptist most poetically as one who witnessed for the Light. This apostle John, the son of Zebedee, said:

"There came a man who was sent from god; his name was John. He came as a witness to testify concerning that light, so that through him all men might believe. He himself was not the light; he came only as a witness to the light."

John 1: 6-8

"John testifies concerning him. He cries out, saying, 'This was he of whom I said', He who comes after me has surpassed me because he was before me.'"

John 1: 15

Again, Jesus is spoken of as One who pre-existed. Actually, John was the older of the two -- Jesus and John. John was born in Judaea five months before Jesus' birth in Bethlehem. But John, because he was given foreknowledge, tells here that Jesus *"was before me,"* surely speaking of Him as the Messiah Who always was and always will be.

"From the fullness of his grace we have all received one blessing after another. For the law was given through Moses; grace and truth came through Jesus Christ."

John 1: 16 &17

So John the Baptist was described as a witness for the Light -- Jesus. He tells us that grace and truth came through Jesus. The Pharisees sent men to question John the Baptist, but they were no match for this one filled with the Holy Spirit.

Lord, help our eyes not to dim through the darkness and distractions of this world. Help us to remain focused on the path of Your Light. Bathe us in the warm glow of Your inestimable grace and truth made manifest in Christ's birth at Christmas. Amen.

TWENTIETH DAY IN ADVENT

John 1: 9 -14

John the apostle tells various times that the world had its beginning through Jesus. So, again, there is testimony that Jesus existed long before his birth in Bethlehem -- that He pre-existed before coming down as the divine Infant that first Christmas.

> "The true light that gives light to every man was coming into the world. He was in the world, and although the world was made through him, the world did not recognize him. He came to that which was his own, but his own did not receive him. Yet to all who received him, to those who believed in his name, he gave the right to become children of God -- children not born of natural descent, nor of human decision or a husband's will, but born of God."
>
> John 1: 9 -13

Here also John tells in essence the story of Jesus' coming. That He entered the world -- His world, His domain -- but was not accepted. But that, in spite of this, He came and offered (offers) a fantastic gift to those who did (do) accept Him -- the power to become "children of God." How beyond belief is the wonder of this great and magnificent gift -- too great for humans to even begin to comprehend. John further describes this:

> "The Word became flesh and made his dwelling among us. We have seen his glory, the glory of the One and Only, who came from the Father, full of grace and truth"
>
> John 1: 14

Lord, You Who were from before the beginnings of time, through Whom all things that are good came to be -- You Who are the Light of the world -- hear our prayer. Please grant us the eyes to see Your Light and the will and the grace to follow it home to be with You always -- now, and forevermore. Amen.

TWENTY-FIRST DAY IN ADVENT

Matthew 22: 37 - 40; Exodus 20: 1 - 17

During Advent, it is good to look inward. Before the holy anniversary of Christ's birth, it is important to look deeply inside, examining our consciences, then ask forgiveness and search hard, seeking His will for our lives.

Jesus told, very simply, usually in a way easy to understand, what He wanted of us. This He did in his two New Testament Commandments.

"Love the Lord your God with all your heart and with all your soul and with all your mind. This is the first and greatest commandment. And the second is like it: Love your neighbor as yourself. All the Law and the Prophets hang on these two commandments."

Matthew 22: 37 - 40

All of the Ten Commandments, as He said, *"hang on these two."* The first five of the Ten Commandments have to do with our love and respect for God; and the last five of those Commandments tell of loving our neighbor as ourselves. If we keep these two Commandments of Jesus, then it follows that the Ten Commandments will be kept.

The first of Jesus' Commandments would have us love Him wholeheartedly and with all our might. In doing this, surely a little of the reflection of His love for us will shine on others, making His second Commandment easier.

The second of Jesus' Commandments -- "You must love your neighbor as yourself" -- seems sometimes misunderstood. True love is an unselfish thing; loving one is to wish and seek always that which is best for that person without seeking selfish gratification.

Lord, how can we cleanse ourselves as John urged us? Without Your grace, we know it is impossible, but with You all things are possible. You, Who are Love Manifest, commanded that we love You with all our hearts, souls and minds and our neighbor as ourselves, yet we frequently fail. We've not always honored Your name. We've not always kept the Sabbath holy. Sometimes we've offended our parents, yielded to anger, hatred and evil thoughts toward others. We've been jealous and envious. And neither have we loved our neighbors as ourselves. Help us to mend our ways, to be heartily sorry for our failings; forgive us Lord, that we may be better persons more pleasing to You Who are All-Good, deserving of all our love. Amen.

AGNUS DEI (13)

Lamb of God, You Who take away the sins of the world, have mercy on us.
Lamb of God, You Who take away the sins of the world, have mercy on us.
Lamb of God, You Who take away the sins of the world, grant us peace.

(c) Catholic Book Publishing Company
All rights reserved.

TWENTY-SECOND DAY IN ADVENT
FOURTH SUNDAY IN WESTERN ADVENT

Romans 12: 8; Matthew 6: 3; Luke 6: 38

Who is this St. Nicholas so respected and admired that, even today, as St. Nick (or as in the colloquial Dutch derivation, Santa Claus), he is remembered as the popular gift-giver at Christmas-time?

"... if it is showing mercy, let him do it cheerfully."

Romans 12: 8

St. Nicholas lived in Myra, a city in Lycia (now modern-day Turkey) during the early Fourth-Century. He was imprisoned and tortured for his faith by the Roman Emperor Diocletian, but later freed by Emperor Constantine after the latter's famous Edict allowing freedom of worship.

Nicholas was born of a noble family, but used his wealth in caring for the poor. A story tells that Nicholas once heard of a destitute man who, in desperation, was about to turn his daughters into a life of shame because there was no money for dowries. So one night Nicholas threw a bag of gold through the poor man's window, and soon the eldest daughter was happily married.

"But when you give to the needy, do not let your left hand know what your right hand is doing, so that your giving may be in secret. Then your Father, who sees what is done in secret, will reward you."

Matthew 6: 3

Nicholas later threw two other bags of gold into that same window until all of the poor man's daughters were safely wed.

Other stories abound about the good that St. Nicholas did. He interceded for three men imprisoned falsely. They were released and then imprisoned again. Finally, Nicholas appeared in a dream to Constantine, and the prisoners were released once and for all, with the Emperor sending a letter asking for prayers for the peace of the world. After death, stories tell that Nicholas' embalmed body gave off a sweet-smelling, healing fragrance.

"Give and it will be given to you. A good measure, pressed down, shaken together and running over, will be poured into your lap. For with the measure you use, it will be measured to you."

Luke 6: 38

Lord, as we gather humble gifts in minute remembrance of the most magnificent, divine Gift of Your beloved Son, let us not forget to give to those in real need as St. Nicholas did so long ago. Let us give secretly as he did, knowing that this is how You said it should be done. Help us to give of ourselves to those in need always, not just during this or that season of the year. We ask in the holy Name of Jesus. Amen.

TWENTY-THIRD DAY IN ADVENT

Isaiah 11: 1 - 4; II Samuel 7: 12 &13; Matthew 1:1

The prophet Isaiah describes what has become known as *"The Jesse Tree."*

"A shoot will come up from the stump of Jesse;
from his roots a Branch will bear fruit
The Spirit of the Lord will rest on him --
the Spirit of wisdom and understanding,
the Spirit of counsel and of power,
the Spirit of knowledge and of the fear of the Lord --
and he will delight in the fear of the Lord.
He will not judge by what he sees with his eyes,
or decide by what he hears with his ears;
but with righteousness he will judge the needy,

with justice he will give decisions for the poor of the earth,
He will strike the earth with the rod of his mouth;
with the breath of his lips he will slay the wicked."

Isaiah 11: 1 - 4

Jesus descended from Jesse through King David, Jesse's son. For centuries, creative people have depicted this symbolic tree in various forms of art, showing Jesus as the final flower springing from the root of Jesse through David and Mary.

God, through Nathan, revealed to David:

"When your days are over and you rest with your fathers, I will raise up your offspring to succeed you, who will come from your own body, and I will establish his kingdom. He is the one who will build a house for my Name, and I will establish the throne of his kingdom forever."

II Samuel 7: 12-13

That throne, secure forever, through the *"Son of David"* --- Christ our Lord.

And in the first sentence of the New Testament, years later, Matthew said:

"A record of the geneology of Jesus Christ the Son of David, the son of Abraham: ... ."

Matthew 1: 1

Again, Lord, You revealed through centuries of fulfilled prophecy, the coming at Christmastime of this Son of David, the ultimate flower of the tree of Jesse. You bring us the King of kings as a tiny Child -- mysterious, grand and holy. Again, You reveal and fulfill and give us beautiful visions of Your divine and heavenly history. Oh Lord Jesus, Son of God and heir to David's throne which shall be forever, forgive our sins and hear our prayer: Allow us to live with You in Your heavenly kingdom forevermore. Amen.

A ROSE-TREE (14)

I know a rose-tree springing
Forth from an ancient root,
As men of old were singing.
From Jesse came the shoot
That bore a blossom bright
Amid the cold of winter,
When half-spent was the night.

This rose-tree, blossom-laden,
Whereof Isaiah spake,
Is Mary, spotless maiden,
Who mothered for our sake,
The little Child, new-born
By God's eternal counsel
On that first Christmas morn.

O flower, whose fragrance tender
With sweetness fills the air,
Dispel in glorious splendor
The darkness everywhere;
True man, yet very God,
From sin and death now save us,
And share our every load. Amen.

German 1599[8]

---

[8] First published in Cologne in 1600, the words are taken from the first verse of the eleventh chapter of Isaiah: "A shoot springs from the stock of Jesse, a scion thrusts from his roots... ."

TWENTY-FOURTH DAY IN ADVENT

Genesis 3:15; Revelation 12:13, 14 &17
Galatians 4: 4 - 7; Romans 16: 20

After the serpent tempted Eve and she tempted Adam and they ate of the forbidden fruit, God told the serpent:

"And I will put enmity between you and the woman,
and between your offspring and hers;
he will crush your head, and you will strike his heel."

Genesis 3: 15

This Hebrew text from Genesis hints at the salvation that Jesus brought. It appears to speak of ultimate victory over Satan. New Testament stories, written thousands of years after these prophecies, echo the same.

For example. the following story is told:

"When the dragon saw that he had been hurled to the earth, he pursued the woman who had given birth to the male child. The woman was given the two wings of a great eagle, so that she might fly to the place prepared for her in the desert, where she would be taken care of for a time ... . Then the dragon was enraged at the woman and went off to make war against the rest of her offspring -- those who obey God's commandments and hold to the testimony of Jesus."

Revelation 12: 13, 14 &17

And Paul, in his letter to the Galatians, said:

"But when the time had fully come, God sent his Son, born of a woman, born under law, to redeem those under law, that we might receive the full rights of sons. Because you are sons, God sent the Spirit of his Son into our hearts, the Spirit who calls out, 'Abba, Father.' So you are no longer a slave, but a son; and since you are a son, God has also made you an heir."

Galatians 4: 4-7

And also in the New Testament:

"The God of peace will soon crush Satan under your feet. The grace of our Lord Jesus be with you."

Romans 16: 20

O Lord God, our heavenly Father, You Who gave us a Redeemer in the Christmas Gift of Jesus to crush the head of Satan who daily torments us, help us as we flounder in this world of sin. Lift us up by the grace of Jesus and give us strength to overcome the power of darkness. Please come to our rescue with the holy Light of Your beloved Son this holy Advent season, surrounding us with the glow and glory of Christmas, now and always. Amen.

THE LEGEND OF THE HOLLY (15)

There is a legend that the holly
wound 'round His head,
and great drops of crimson blood
against the green, they bled.

The holly mocked, as if a crown
of laurel for a king;
yet intertwined were cruel thorns
that pierced -- a blood-let ring.

The sharp pain tore His tender brow,
but that was only part; --
for penetrating, O, so deep --
it broke His tender heart.

The Father said, 'Forevermore
the holly tree shall bear
crimson berries with the green
like laid once in His hair.

And thorns would never form again
upon the holly tree,
but berries red, and prickly leaves
would be for all to see.'

> At Christmastide the wreaths are formed
> of holly green and red --
> reminder of what our dear Lord
> had wound 'round His head.

TWENTY-FIFTH DAY IN ADVENT

Psalm 110: 1 - 4

Again, a Psalmist of the Old Testament predicts the coming of the Kingly Christ.

> *"Sit at my right hand until I make your enemies*
> *a footstool for your feet.*
> *The Lord will extend your mighty scepter from Zion;*
> *you will rule in the midst of your enemies.*
> *Your troops will be willing on your day of battle.*
> *Arrayed in holy majesty, from the womb of the dawn*
> *you will receive the dew of your youth.*
> *The Lord has sworn and will not change his mind:*
> *'You are a priest forever, ...'"*
>
> Psalm 110: 1 - 4

Interestingly, not only prophesies from the Holy Scriptures seem to speak of Christ. Virgil, the Roman poet, before Christ's birth in about 30 BC, wrote in his ECOLOGUE IV:

> *"The last great Age, foretold by sacred Rhymes,*
> *Renews its finish'd Course, Saturnian times*
> *Rowl round again, and mighty years, begun*
> *From their first Orb, in radiant Circles run.*
> *The base degen'rate Iron-off-spring ends;*
> *A golden Progeny from Heav'n descends.*
> *O chast Lucina speed the Mother's pains;*
> *And haste the glorious Birth ... !" (16)*

Many prophetic visions point to Jesus. He is spoken of in many ways, such as the Messiah, the Savior, the King, the Lamb, the Son of Man and the Son of God. And, as Virgil said, *"A Golden Prodigy from heav'n descends."*

In these days, Lord, of eager expectation and awesome anticipation, prepare our hearts for the anniversary of Your unspeakably wonderful Gift. Help us to cope with the complexities of life by fixing our minds and hearts on You. Wrap us in Your love, Lord, as we draw nearer this holy season. And send Your holy angels to guide us home some day to be with You forever. Amen.

THE BABY'S FORE'D (17)

The Baby's fore'd was made
for thorns.
Those chubby hands
for nails.
'Tis Bethlehem, plus
Calvary
Where God's real love
unveils... .

Author unknown

TWENTY-SIXTH DAY IN ADVENT

Psalm 1: 1 & 2; Revelation 22: 14

"Blessed is the man who does not walk in the council of the wicked or stand in the way of sinners or sit in the seat of mockers. But his delight is in the law of the Lord, and on his law he meditates day and night."

Psalm 1: 1 & 2

Today we see garlanded trees everywhere. The season of Advent is filled with merriment -- the joy of Jesus' coming that surrounds them. Evergreen trees are symbols of eternity, ever green, never browning nor dying out in winter. They can also be symbols of that other tree, the one that formed a cross at Calvary from which the Baby's chubby hands-now-grown-to-manhood hung from acrid blood-stained nails for our sin.

The Holy Scriptures tell of still another tree:

"Blessed are those who wash their robes, that they may have the right to the tree of life and may go through the gates into the city."

Revelation 22: 14

Lord, help us by Your grace to *"wash [our] robes"* so that we may have the right, bought by You, to feed on the Tree of Life. Allow us during this sometimes desecrated season of parties and tinsel trees, to see the evergreen and think of You -- forever living and offering eternal life. May we *"not walk in the council of the wicked or stand in the way of sinners or sit in the seat of mockers"*. But may we meditate on Your holy Law, on Your Word, seeking to align our will with Yours, day and night, that by Your grace and tender mercies, we may draw nearer to You this holy season and always. Amen.

TWENTY-SEVENTH DAY IN ADVENT

Numbers 6: 24 - 26; Psalm 67: 1 & 2; Philippians 2: 14 & 16

It is as if, during the Advent season and at Christmas, God lets His "face shine" on us -- makes His face smile on us.

*"The Lord bless you and keep you;
the Lord make his face shine upon you
and be gracious to you;
the Lord turn his face toward you
and give you peace."*

Numbers 6: 24 - 26

*"May God be gracious to us and bless us
and make his face shine upon us, Selah
that your ways may be known on earth,
your salvation among all nations."*

Psalm 67: 1 & 2

A non-Christian friend came to me during the Christmas season, her own face quixotically warm. She said, "It is as if everywhere I go, I see -- as if the whole world is blanketed in this warm glow... ."

One sees more warm smiles at Christmas than at any other time. Even in the hectic bustle of Christmas shopping there seem to be Mona Lisa smiles on people standing in lines, at check-out counters, sloshing through the snow, or kneeling in church. It is the season of sharing, of experiencing that especial joy that comes with unselfish giving-to-others. As if we, in our finite way, are trying to reflect an iota of God's inimitable sharing of the Greatest Gift -- Jesus.

In Paul's letter to the Philippians, he said:

"Do everything without complaining or arguing, so that you may become blameless and pure, children of God without fault in a crooked and depraved generation, in which you shine like stars in the universe as you hold out the word of life. ... ."

Philippians 2: 14 & 16

Lord, let us shine to those who do not know You. Let us in some way, by Your grace, reflect to others the brilliance of Your smile on us at Christmas, now and always. Help us to be reflections, however small, of Your Great-Good-Love. Amen.

DAY BY DAY (18)

Day by Day,
Dear Lord of Thee three things I pray:
To see Thee more clearly,
Love Thee more dearly,
Follow Thee more nearly,
Day by day.

Richard of Chichester[9]
1199-1253

---

[9] Richard of Chichester denied himself riches, from his inheritance as well as from other sources. Throughout his lifetime as a priest and bishop, he shared what he had with the poor. His aim throughout life was to imitate the life of Jesus as much as was in his capacity to do.

TWENTY-EIGHTH DAY IN ADVENT

1 Peter 5: 7; Psalm 55: 22

Because Jesus came into the world, we are able to better know Him and cast our cares on Him.

"Cast all your anxiety on him because he cares for you."

1 Peter 5:7

What comfortable words that we may unload all our worries upon Him -- all our cares, troubles and concerns --*"because he cares for"* us. He, who is all-powerful and all-wise.

How simple this seems; yet, really, it is not so easily done. Once, when in deep worry and concern over a member of my family, and when praying hard about it all, a friend admonished me sharply.

"You are not casting your care upon Jesus. You take it to His feet and then bring it back!"

Oh, I was praying, very fervently. But I was showing it to Him, and then holding onto it as if I, alone, could solve the seemingly impossible problem.

"Cast all your anxiety on him because he cares for you."

1 Peter 5:7

I should have taken my care to Him in prayer, and then listened for direction. And after that, when I had done all that reasonably could have been done to remedy the situation, I should have unloaded all my worries on to Him with thanksgiving. *Then,* I should have relaxed in trust and faith.

"Cast your cares on the Lord and he will sustain you; he will never let the righteous fall."

Psalm 55: 22

Thank you, dearest Jesus, for always being there for us, no matter when or where or how difficult the problem. Help us to have the complete faith to take all of our concerns to You, leaving them at Your feet in prayer. Amen.

TWENTY-NINTH DAY IN ADVENT

Philippians 2: 6 - 8; Matthew 5: 44, 7: 1 - 5 ; Proverbs 16: 5

What is humility, that He should value it so? That our very God would deign to leave His Heavenly home and subject Himself to such a lowly estate, is almost incomprehensible.

But He did. Throughout His life He frowned on those with haughty looks. He set the example of basest humility, this God-coming-to-earth, born in a stable with dumb animals and laid in their feeding trough.

"Who, being in very nature God,
did not consider equality with God
something to be grasped, but made himself nothing,
taking the very nature of servant,
being made in human likeness.
And being found in appearance as a man,
he humbled himself and became obedient to death --
even death on a cross!"

Philippians 2: 6 - 8

If He can so humble Himself by birth on earth, submitting Himself to human degradation, severe torture and death for us -- this world's sinful people -- can I not humble myself? Have I the right to pride?

Thinking on this tiny Baby-God, born in a manger, I wonder at how He set the example. He washed feet; He acted as a servant and said for us to do the same. He said to love my neighbor as myself. He didn't say for me to sit in judgment on them. He even told us to love -- really, truly love -- our enemies.

"But I tell you: Love your enemies and pray for those who persecute you... ."

Matthew 5: 44

I have tried and failed to love my enemies, then I learned how to do this seemingly impossible thing. Jesus plainly said to "pray for those who persecute you." And I learned that it works magnificently; after I have prayed for my enemies, the love comes!

> "Do not judge, or you too will be judged. For in the same way you judge others, you will be judged, and with the measure you use, it will be measured to you. Why do you look at the speck of sawdust in your brother's eye and pay no attention to the plank in your own eye? How can you say to your brother, 'Let me take the speck out of your eye,' when all the time there is a plank in your own eye? You hypocrite, first take the plank out of your own eye, and then you will see clearly to remove the speck from your brother's eye."
>
> Matthew 7: 1 - 5

How plainly He said this, our Lord -- our dear Baby-Jesus-grown-to-manhood and become the Teacher-of-teachers, the Lord-of-hosts, our all-wise, all-loving Christ-God-Messiah.

> "The Lord detests all the proud of heart. Be sure of this: they will not go unpunished."
>
> Proverbs 16: 5

Dearest Lord Jesus, shame our proud hearts; humble us; help us to see ourselves in all our sinfulness; let us know and feel great remorse and true contrition; and show us how to truly love our enemies, by praying for them first. Then, humbled, may we come to You and ask Your divine forgiveness. In Jesus' Name, Amen.

THIRTIETH DAY IN ADVENT

Philippians 4: 6, 7 & 9

There are passages in Paul's letter to the Philippians that offer tremendous peace -- the peace that Jesus gives.

> "... whatever is true, whatever is noble, whatever is right, whatever is pure, whatever is lovely, whatever is admirable -- if anything is excellent or praiseworthy -- think about such things."
>
> Philippians 4: 8

If, at least for an Advent season and hopeful thereby forming a lifetime habit, we can fill our minds with these thoughts, what a rewarding experience will follow! Grumbling and anger, worry and apprehension, jealousy and hate -- all these negative feelings would be tamed - negated - as positive feelings would so fill our beings that there would hardly be room for anything else.

Everything that is good -- what is noble, right, pure, lovely, admirable, excellent and praiseworthy -- these would fill our minds and therefore our hearts.

In this world, how difficult it is to think always on what is good and positive. How selective one must be in media choices, for example, to do this. We are constantly bombarded on all sides by the opposite. Evil is presented as good, and good presented as evil. Those who would live by His law are often made to look ludicrous; those who live against His law are often made to look admirable. To obey the seemingly simple task of this biblical passage seems almost impossible, yet with God all things are possible.

We are given a wonderful promise if we keep our minds on good things. Paul's letter to the Philippians also says:

"Do not be anxious about anything, but in everything, by prayer and petition, with thanksgiving, present your requests to God. And the peace of God, which transcends all understanding, will guard your hearts and minds in Christ Jesus. ... And the God of peace will be with you."

Philippians 4: 6, 7 & 9

Holy Lord, bless our efforts this Advent season to draw nearer to You. Cleanse us and fill our hearts, minds and souls with what is true, noble, honorable and virtuous. By Your gracious tender mercies, enfold us in Your Love and righteousness. Amen.

THIRTY-FIRST DAY IN ADVENT

Revelation 3: 20; Psalm 27: 4-6

During this time of awaiting the anniversary of Jesus' coming to earth, it is good to think long and often on its meaning. By His willingness to come, He opened the doors to hope for us; He opened the doors to eternal life; He allowed us to know Him, to approach Him -- to love Him.

> "Here I am! I stand at the door and knock. If anyone hears my voice and opens the door, I will come in ... ."
>
> Revelation 3: 20

> "One thing I ask of the Lord,
> this is what I seek:
> that I may dwell in the house of the Lord
> all the days of my life,
> to gaze upon the beauty of the Lord
> and to seek him in his temple.
> For in the day of trouble
> he will keep me safe in his dwelling;
> he will hide me in the shelter of his tabernacle
> and set me high upon a rock.
> Then my head will be exhalted
> above the enemies who surround me;
> at his tabernacle will I sacrifice with shouts of joy;
> I will sing and make music to the Lord."
>
> Psalm 27: 4-6

Some days I feel so stressed, bowed down with trouble; sometimes it is as if I am struggling with seemingly insurmountable problems; it is as if I am sinking, and there seems to be no one to help nor to care nor understand; other times there is great danger, and my enemies are very real.

In such days I run to Him; He is always there; He enfolds me in His love; He holds me and cares for me; He hides me in His secret place; He allows me to rest, and He comforts me. He wipes away my tears, and makes me glad, and touches me with happiness and joy. He gives me back my strength, picking me up, and setting me on the straight way, allowing me to smile again.

Lord, one thing we ask -- one thing we seek: to live in Your house all the days of our lives. Amen.

THIRTY-SECOND DAY IN ADVENT

Genesis 1:1; Job 12:10; Nehemiah 9: 6
Psalm 102: 25 - 27; John 1:1-5

From the beginnings of the written word until the present time, throughout place to the ends of the earth, man has proclaimed that there is a God. He is described in magnificent terms. Yet, He took on our humanity and came into the world to be with us. Here are descriptions of Him, this great-good Lord, very Love yet very God, Who came down to earth, born in a manger. The following words span millenniums, yet speak of the same God with the same attributes.

"In the beginning God created the heavens and the earth."

Genesis 1:1

"In his hand is the life of every creature and the breath of all mankind."

Job 12:10

"You alone are the Lord. You made the heavens, even the highest heavens, and all their starry host, the earth and all that is on it, the seas and all that is in them. You gave life to everything... ."

Nehemiah 9: 6

"In the beginning you laid the foundations of the earth,
and the heavens are the work of your hands.
They will perish but you remain;
they will all wear out like a garment. ...
But you remain the same,
and your years will never end."

Psalm 102: 25-27

"In the beginning was the Word:
the Word was with God and the Word was God.
He was with God in the beginning.
Through him all things were made;
without him nothing was made that has been made.
In him was life, and that life was the light of men.
The light shines in the darkness, but the darkness has not understood it."

John 1: 1-5

These statements were made by different people during vastly different times from the beginnings of recorded history, each agreeing with the other about our Lord. They span thousands of years, these corroborating statements. How can I not believe and be humbled by all this testimony to the universal belief about the majesty of the mighty Creator-God?

There are those who contend that all things just happened, that there was no Creator. Yet man in all his scientific genius has never found a way to create life from nothing. Only from life comes life. In essence, there must be a First Cause -- a First Life.

The intricate perfection of the human body with all its complexity astounds. Consider this: should *all* its parts be broken down into chemical substances (so much matter consisting of H2O etc.), and all these substances placed in a container -- how long, how many years, centuries or eons would pass before they would evolve (assemble themselves) into a living human being? Indeed -- could it *ever* happen? Could anything of such complex ordered perfection have happened by itself -- randomly?

To look at a newborn baby, or the perfection of a rose -- to look at the cloudless star-filled sky or experience a dawn or sunset -- each perennially renewing in orderly fashion -- is only to perceive in the minutest way, a glimpse of the shadow of His handiwork.

And yet God, in all His glory, sent His only begotten Son, very God, to earth to be born of Mary.

Lord God, Heavenly Father, Almighty and All-Powerful Lord, You Who created the heavens and the earth and all that is within them, thank You for allowing us the gift of knowing You. Thank You for allowing us in our insignificance the ability to come to You in prayer. Thank You for sending us the unspeakably wonderful Gift of Your dearly beloved Son, precious Jesus. Amen.

THIRTY-THIRD DAY IN ADVENT

Jeremiah 23: 5 & 6

Again, a prophecy of the Messiah -- this time by the prophet Jeremiah six hundred years before Jesus' birth. Again, it is prophesied that a virtuous branch of David will be raised up. The term *"Branch"* became a title for the Messiah -- Jesus, the Christ-Child born in Bethlehem.

"'The days are coming,' declares the Lord, 'when I will raise up to David a righteous Branch,
a King who will reign wisely
and do what is just and right in the land. ...
This is the name by which he will be called: The Lord Our Righteousness.'"

Jeremiah 23: 5 & 6

We are almost there -- to the time of the celebration of the Messiah's coming. The time is short; the anxiety great.

Cleanse us, O Precious Jesus-Lord-Our-Righteousness. Make our hearts new, ready to receive the wonder of Your birth. In Your holy Name we ask: humble us, forgive us, make us clean by the grace of Your Love. In these days of hectic tension, help us to cope. May we do better in all You would have us do. Give us patience, Lord, with all we encounter daily; free us from sloth and clumsy error; help us to love and forgive; grant us strength and wisdom to overcome temptation and to set a good example. Purify us, Lord, that we may draw nearer to You as Your holy season draws close to the divine birthday. Amen.

THIRTY-FOURTH DAY IN ADVENT

Matthew 6: 3 & 4; 25: 40

The Magi brought their fine presents to baby Jesus -- gold, frankincense and myrrh. There is much written about bringing gifts to God. Yet there is a secret way to bring something to Jesus which takes only a little time yet it can have wonderful results; it is by offering secret prayers for strangers.

"But when you give to the needy, do not let your left hand know what your right hand is doing, so that your giving may be in secret. Then your Father, who sees what is done in secret, will reward you."

Matthew 6: 3 & 4

In this busy life of stress and tension, there is a simple way to bring peace and tranquillity; it is by praying privately and secretly for perfect strangers who are completely unaware of what is happening. There are many little times scattered throughout a day which could be breeding times for worry -- traffic snarls, waiting in line (or waiting wherever), tedious chores, dealing with difficulties.

At such times, it is good to single out a person one doesn't personally know, perhaps someone standing at a bus stop, or in a check-out counter, or someone passing on the street, or just someone noticed in the mind's eye from a recent memory, and ask God's blessings on that person. An even better idea is to do this for someone who has offended in some way.

Such a prayer might be phrased this way: *"In the name of the Father, the Son and the Holy Spirit, please forgive my sins and hear my prayer. Bless that man with the stooped back. Relieve his pains of body and spirit and draw him close to You. Help him with his deepest problems and enfold him in Your gracious love, now and forever. Amen."* Or, simply, "God bless that lady." There are many ways to say such a prayer.

It is scientifically known that prayer lowers blood pressure and relieves stress. Who can say what great good might come from this simple practice, to the giver and to the receiver? Our Lord told us to give and to pray and His reasons are beyond understanding, yet always perfect. As Tennyson said, *"There are more things wrought by prayer than this world dreams of."* (19)

One cannot bring good to another without receiving some personally. Love cannot be shared unless it's owned; it cannot be handled without being touched. To immerse another in it, means to be immersed -- immersed in love. He gave us the example -- His great profound love -- and He said to care for one's neighbors.

> *"I tell you the truth, whatever you did for one of the least of these brothers of mine, you did for me."*
>
> Matthew 25: 40

Dear Father in Heaven, forgive our sins and hear our prayer. Bless all in the world who suffer for whatever reason. Alleviate their pain. Let them seek Your will, feel Your presence and be consoled by Your tender mercies. We ask in the name of Jesus. Amen.

Thirty-Fifth Day in Advent

Acts 17: 23 & 28; 1 John 4: 8

By coming to earth, our Lord showered us with Love, a Love we were unable to comprehend then as now in its fullness, but never-the-less, a boundless, inscrutable Love made manifest to us.

Paul, when passing through Greece, came upon an altar with the following words inscribed:

"TO AN UNKNOWN GOD."

Acts 17: 23

Paul then began telling the people about this *"Unknown God"* who made the heavens and the earth and all that is in them. "For *in him we live and move and have our being ... ."* he told them. (Acts 17: 28)

Because Jesus came to earth, we are able to know Him better, to learn of and from Him, to share His love with others, and to follow Him more closely. Before He came, it was hard to understand His great, fathomless and incomprehensible compassion. Even after He came and demonstrated it to us, we see, we feel, we know -- yet it is impossible to fully comprehend.

"... God is love."

1 John 4: 8

How often we in this imperfect world seek a perfect love. We give our hearts to this or that person, and we expect perfect understanding and are sometimes terribly hurt when it is not returned. We yearn for and expect to be loved, unconditionally. Yet among humans this is impossible. Even as parents, children, husbands, wives, and friends, we love deeply, yet at times, in our humanness, we fail those who are dearest to us. He alone knows us in our entirety, yet never ever fails to return our love. He alone sees us with all our faults -- all our blemishes and shortcomings -- yet loves us more dearly than we can ever comprehend.

Dearest Lord Jesus, Heavenly Father, and Holy Spirit, help us in some way, however minute, to know and understand You better -- to feel Your inestimable Love. And help us to share this, neither expecting nor asking its return, but freely giving this compassion that You so freely give to us. May we be heartily sorry for offending You Who are all-perfect and all-holy, so that we may ask forgiveness and draw closer to You, enfolded in Your boundless compassion and tender mercies. Amen.

THIRTY-SIXTH DAY IN ADVENT

Matthew 6: 9-13 - 15; John 6: 35; Romans 14:17

This Advent, as we attempt to prepare ourselves for the symbolic coming again of Christ on His birthday, it is good to try to better understand the prayer He gave us.

"Our Father in heaven,
hallowed be your name,
your kingdom come,
your will be done on earth as it is in heaven.
Give us today our daily bread.
Forgive us our debts,
as we also have forgiven our debtors.
And lead us not into temptation,
but deliver us from the evil one."

Matthew 6: 9-13

Always it has been cherished, this Lord's Prayer. It has been said in private and in public, in the most pained and in the happiest of times; it has been recited in unison by great masses of people and it has been whispered silently, imploringly, by those alone; it has been, is now and always shall be loved by all Christendom and is one of the few things cherished by all those who profess Christ. It is the dearest prayer, yet it has been said that familiarity breeds contempt, and somehow, the Lord's Prayer has been taken for granted by many of us.

Jesus said that this was the way we should pray. As we say *"Our Father in heaven,..."* we can visualize this contact with the all-Father, the triune God in heaven -- the perfect place of eternal happiness. This very first phrase verifies that there *is* a God and that there *is* a heaven and that we can actually communicate with God in heaven. What follows, *"... hallowed be your name,"* sets this Being apart as holy, sacred and due the highest honor.

Advent Anticipation: Drawing Nearer to the Christ-Child

"Your kingdom come,..." is a request of the greatest order; if His kingdom comes to us, for what more could we ever hope? All that is of any importance would be realized. Paul said that the kingdom of God is about *"...righteousness, peace and joy in the Holy Spirit,"* (Romans 14: 17) If it is a Kingdom of God, then His will would be done. What a perfect wish! *"... your will be done on earth as it is in heaven... ."* We may have in mind to pray for specific people or many, yet here, with these eleven words, we can visualize the world and all its people and God's will being done to each.

"... Give us today our daily bread. ... ." If one has in mind to ask God to provide daily needs, it is said here. What is meant by *"bread?"* One meaning is whatever we have need of in our lives. It also represents Jesus himself. *"I am the bread of life. He who comes to me will never go hungry, and he who believes in me will never be thirsty."* (John 6: 35)

"Forgive us our debts, as we also have forgiven our debtors." This is the hard part, yet if He can forgive us, how can we not forgive others? He then admonishes, *"For if you forgive men when they sin against you, your heavenly Father will also forgive you. But if you do not forgive men their sins, your Father will not forgive your sins."* (Matthew 6:14 & 15)

"And lead us not into temptation, but deliver us from the evil one." Here it ends so reassuringly. Lord, it says, let us not be tempted and protect us from evil. What more could one ask or need or wish for in this universe?

> *"Our Father in heaven, hallowed be your name, your kingdom come, your will be done on earth as it is in heaven.*
> *Give us today our daily bread. Forgive us our debts, as we also have forgiven our debtors. And lead us not into temptation, but deliver us from the evil one."*
>
> Amen.

THIRTY-SEVENTH DAY IN ADVENT

Matthew 11: 28 - 30

This Christ, the holy infant born in Bethlehem, gave us such sweet, profound promises.

He once said:

"Come to me, all you who are weary and burdened, and I will give you rest. Take my yoke upon you and learn from me, for I am gentle and humble in heart, and you will find rest for your souls. For my yoke is easy and my burden is light"

Matthew 11: 28 - 30

This is God Who created the heavens and the earth, Maker of the universe, talking to us. Hear Him, our Lord God, saying, *"I am gentle and humble in heart... ."*

When we are tired, worried, with problems almost beyond our power to bear, we can think on this. How often there is the striving and the conflict and there are the terrible problems that come into our lives. Yet how simply He states what He would have us do.

When yoked with Him there will ever be the closeness. It means that He, the Almighty God, will pull with us in our daily grind and in our going forward. He said that His burden is easy and light.

Somehow, though, it seems hard because confusions of the world get in the way. Yet He who is all-powerful, who created the world itself, would carry our problems for us.

He said to come to Him, all of us who work and feel heaviness of life, and He will give us rest. He said to learn of Him, that He is meek and the opposite of proud. And He said He will give our souls rest. He offers us this grand sweet gift, yet we often struggle on through life as if we, alone, can bear our burdens.

Loving Jesus, help us to humbly and with thanksgiving accept Your precious and most gracious gifts. Help us to learn to share our pains and other burdens with You. How can we comprehend and thank You Who are very God, offering to bend down, stooping from Your place in Paradise, to the lowest level on earth to touch us, sinful as we are, to shoulder our burdens, lifting our pitiful problems and miseries from us? By Your grace, teach us to trust in You Who daily enfold us in Your tender mercies. Amen.

THIRTY-EIGHTH DAY IN ADVENT

Philippians 4: 6,7 & 9; John 14: 27

Jesus brought to earth His wonderful gift of the peace that passes understanding. Paul, in his letter to the Philippians, said:

"Do not be anxious about anything, but in everything, by prayer and petition, with thanksgiving, present your requests to God. And the peace of God, which transcends all understanding, will guard your hearts and your minds in Christ Jesus. ... the God of peace will be with you."

Philippians 4: 6, 7 & 9

The God of peace, through Paul, tells us not to worry. He tells us to simply pray for whatever we need, asking with thanksgiving, and He assures us of a peace that is beyond comprehension.

I notice something here that may be a key. How seldom my prayers include thanksgiving. And yet, Paul said: *"... by prayer and petition, with thanksgiving present your requests to God."* How often I take His manifold blessings, His love, for granted.

He promises a wonderful peace, but we are told to pray with *thanksgiving.* Perhaps the thanksgiving would not have to be uttered within the prayer, if that prayer is offered with a truly thankful heart. *Then* we are promised this peace beyond anything imaginable that will guard our hearts and thoughts in Christ Jesus.

"Peace I leave with you; my peace I give you. I do not give to you as the world gives. Do not let your hearts be troubled and do not be afraid."

John 14: 27

Dear Lord Jesus, forgive our sin and hear our prayer offered with thanksgiving for You, our divine Saviour. Thank You for our manifold blessings, uncountable as the stars that fill the universe -- from times past, from now, and always. Surround us with Your peace that passes all understanding. Dearest Lord Jesus! Amen.

THIRTY-NINTH DAY IN ADVENT

Daniel 2: 31 - 35, 44

Daniel, years before it happened, prophesied of Jesus and the Kingdom of God.

> *"... the God of heaven will set up a kingdom that will never be destroyed, nor will it be left to another people. It will crush all those kingdoms and bring them to an end, but it will itself endure forever."*
>
> Daniel 2: 44

Daniel was asked by the king to tell him the meaning of his dreams. The king's dream was of *"... an enormous, dazzling statue, awesome in appearance. The head of the statue was made of pure gold, its chest and arms of silver, its belly and thighs of bronze, its legs of iron, its feet partly of iron and partly of baked clay."* The statue broke into fine particles and a great wind blew them away, but, finally, the stone *"... grew into a great mountain, filling the earth."*

Daniel 2: 31-35

Daniel prophesied the restoration of the heavenly Kingdom of God, the Kingdom that Jesus spoke of so many times -- the Kingdom not of this world.

> *"... the God of heaven will set up a kingdom that will never be destroyed, ... it will itself endure forever."*
>
> Daniel 2: 44

So many fulfillments of Old Testament prophecy culminated in the coming to earth of Jesus, the tiny Baby-Christ-Child, in Bethlehem.

Dear Lord Jesus, please open our eyes to see You in the many marvels of prophecy, in Your creations, in Your Holy Word, and in our brothers and sisters in their need. Guide us into a closer vision of You. May we, in seeking Your Face, rightly interpret Your will for us, and by Your grace, do as You would have us do in our lives. We ask in Your holy Name, with thanksgiving, praise and love. Amen.

FORTIETH DAY IN ADVENT

John 3: 14 - 16; 10: 27 & 28; 14: 1 - 3; Mark 10: 29 & 30

It is a warm and wonderful thing during the Advent season to think on the sweet sayings of Jesus about eternal life. When He came down from heaven He opened the doors of Paradise. Jesus once said to Nicodemus, a Pharisee:

> *"Just as Moses lifted up the snake in the desert, so the Son of Man must be lifted up, that everyone who believes in him may have eternal life. For God so loved the world that he gave his one and only Son, that whoever believes in him may have eternal life."*
>
> John 3: 14 -16

Jesus talked about how those who have left family and possessions for His sake will have eternal life.

> *"'I tell you the truth,' Jesus replied, 'no one who has left home or brothers or sisters or father or children or fields for me and the gospel will fail to receive a hundred times as much in this present age (homes brothers, sisters, mothers, children and fields -- and with them, persecutions) and in the new age to come, eternal life.'"*
>
> Mark 10: 29 & 30

> *"The sheep listen to my voice;*
> *I know them, and they follow me.*
> *I give them eternal life, ..."*
>
> John 10: 27 & 28

Then there is the passage about Jesus going to prepare a place for us.

> *"Do not let your hearts be troubled. Trust in God; trust also in me. In my Father's house are many rooms; if it were not so, I would have told you. I am going there to prepare a place for you. And if I go and prepare a place for you, I will come back and take you to be with me that you also may be where I am."*
>
> John 14: 1 - 3

This prayer of the late Russian martyr, Alexander Men, spoke also of eternity.

"Grant us, divine Teacher, the strength of ... faith ... and the fire of ... love for You. When we, lost on life's path, stop, not knowing where to go, grant that we might see Your face in the gloom. Through the howling and thundering of this technological age, at once so mighty and so poor and powerless, teach us to attend to the silence of eternity and let us hear in it Your voice, Your courage-instilling words: 'I am with you always, to the close of the age.'" (20) Amen.

(c) Samuel Brown, trans., & Oakwood Pub. 1999
All rights reserved

CHRISTMAS (21)

No love that in a family dwells,
No caroling in frosty air,
Nor all the steeple-shaking bells
Can with this simple truth compare --
That God was Man in Palestine
And lives today in Bread and Wine.

(c) John Betjeman 1970[10]
Used by permission

---

[10] Sir John Betjeman, a high Anglican and 20th century British author of both prose and poetry, was named Poet Laureate in 1972. All rights reserved.

PART III

CHRISTMAS EVE AND THE TWELVE DAYS OF CHRISTMAS

"The Creator shaped man with His own hands,
but when He saw us perishing eternally,
He bowed the heavens and came down to earth,
and clothed Himself completely in our nature,
truly incarnate from a pure and holy Virgin, ..." (22)
from Canon of Cosmas of Maiuma. Ode One[11]

CHRISTMAS EVE

Luke 2: 1-5; John 7:42

The anniversary of the ultimate fulfillment of all the scripture prophecies from the beginnings of time about the coming of the Messiah draws very close -- the coming to earth of the infant Jesus, the Child-God.

"In those days Caesar Augustus issued a decree that a census should be taken of the entire Roman world. (This was the first census that took place

---

[11] Cosmas and his twin bother Damian were born in Arabia but studied the sciences in Syria where they practiced many charitable acts including providing medical treatment without receiving payment. They were beheaded for their faith by Diocletian.

while Quirinius was governor of Syria.) And everyone went to his own town to register. So Joseph also went up from the town of Nazareth in Galilee to Judea, to Bethlehem the town of David, because he belonged to the house and line of David. He went thereto register with Mary who was pledged to be married to him and was expecting a child."

Luke 2: 1-5

"Does not the Scripture say that the Christ will come from David's family and from Bethlehem, the town where David lived?"

John 7: 42

The Virgin, great with Child conceived by the Holy Spirit, and Joseph, the descendent of David, go to the town of Bethlehem from which the Messiah is to come. Shepherds are in the fields nearby, keeping watch over their flocks. A magnificent star forms in the east, attracting attention of Wise Men.

Words fail to describe the wonder and marvel and magnificence of this. Christina Rossetti said it this way:

> "Christmas hath a darkness
> Brighter than the blazing noon,
> Christmas hath a chillness
> Warmer than the heat of June,
> Christmas hath a beauty
> Lovelier than the world can show:
> For Christmas bringeth Jesus,
> Brought for us so low... ." (23)

O Lord, we are poised on this holy and silent night, our minds and souls and hearts drawn to You in the little town of Bethlehem. The anniversary of Your magnificent Gift is awaited in awesome and joyous anticipation. A remote shadow of Your great-good-love is mirrored here on earth by the warmth of the Christmas spirit. We, in our imperfection, attempt however disproportionately, to share, and haltingly to love as You have shared and loved so freely. It is as if now, hands joined around the world in caring, Christians and non-Christians alike approach the eve of the celebration of Your birthday bound by the blessing of the angels two thousand years ago: *"Peace... ."* Cleanse us, O Lord, and grant us, with the help of Your angels so prominent during all aspects of Jesus' birth, to draw nearer to You during this blessed time of Christmas and always. Amen.

O Holy Night (Cantique de Noel) (24)

O holy night! The stars are brightly shining,
It is the night of our dear savior's birth!
Long lay the world in sin and error pining -
Till He appeared, and the soul felt its worth.
A thrill of hope the weary world rejoices,
For yonder breaks a new and glorious morn;
Fall on your knees, Oh, hear the angel voices!
O night divine, O night when Christ was born!
O night, O holy night, O night divine!

French carol[12]
Placide Cappeau De Roquemaure 1847

Christmas Day
First Day of Christmas

Luke 2: 6 & 7; Matthew 1: 22 & 23

Love and joy!
Praise be in heaven and earth for Jesus is born!
Glory to God in the highest!
On earth, peace!

"While they were there the time came for the baby to be born, and she gave birth to her firstborn, a son. She wrapped him in cloths and placed him in a manger, because there was no room for them in the inn."

Luke 2: 6 & 7

---

[12] This poem, translated into English by John S. Dwight, co-founder of the Harvard Music Society, was first written in 1847 by Placide Cappeau, mayor of the French town of Roquemaure.

"All this took place to fulfill what the Lord had said through the prophet:
'The virgin will be with child
and will give birth to a son,
and they will call him 'Immanuel' --
which means, 'God with us.'"

                                                                    Matthew 1: 22 & 23

Love came down from Heaven, the most precious possible Gift from the God of all to us, poor and undeserving as we are.

"Love came down at Christmas,
Love all lovely, Love divine;
Love was born at Christmas,
Star and angels gave the sign.

Worship we the Godhead,
Love incarnate, Love divine;
Worship we our Jesus:
But wherewith for a sacred sign?

Love shall be our token,
Love be yours and love be mine.
Love to God for all men,
Love for plea and gift and sign." (25)

                                                                    Christina Rossetti

Thank You, Lord God -- the Father, Son and Holy Spirit -- thank You Immanuel. Amen.

SILENT NIGHT (26)

Silent night, holy night,
All is calm, all is bright
Round yon virgin mother and Child.
Holy infant so tender and mild,
Sleep in heavenly peace.
Sleep in heavenly peace.

Silent night, holy night,
Shepherd's quake at the sight,
Glories stream from heaven afar,
Heavenly hosts sing alleluia;
Christ the Savior is born!
Christ the Savior is born!

Silent night, holy night,
Son of God, love's pure light
Radiant beams from Thy holy Face,
with the dawn of redeeming grace,
Jesus, Lord, at Thy birth.
Jesus, Lord, at Thy birth.

Joseph Mohr 1818[13]

THE SECOND DAY OF CHRISTMAS

Luke 2: 8-11

The news of the birth of Jesus, the Good Shepherd Who came down in humility, was first announced to the humble shepherds near the little town of Bethlehem.

> *"And there were shepherds living out in the fields nearby, keeping watch over their flocks at night. An angel of the Lord appeared to them, and the glory of the Lord shone around them, and they were terrified. But the angel said to them, 'Do not be afraid. I bring you good news of great joy that will be for all the people. Today in the town of David a Savior has been born to you; he is Christ the Lord. This will be a sign to you: you will find a baby wrapped in cloths and lying in a manger.'"*
>
> Luke 2: 8-11

---

[13] In the small village of Oberdorf, high in the Austrian Alps, a Catholic priest by the name of Joseph Mohr composed these words on the afternoon of December 24, 1818. The church organ was broken, so the church organist, Franz Gruber, set the words to a simple tune appropriate for two singers and a guitar. So on that night, during midnight Mass, this famous Christmas carol was born.

Jesus, the Lamb of God Who came down from above as the most magnificent Gift -- Jesus, the Paschal Lamb -- was, indeed, as prophesied of old, born in Bethlehem.

Lambs have long been symbols of sacrifice as well as what is gentle, meek and mild. The eighteenth century English poet and artist, William Blake, referred to this in his poem, "The Lamb." (27)

"Little Lamb, who made thee?
Dost thou know who made thee?
Gave thee life, and bid thee feed,
By the stream and o'er the mead?
Gave thee clothing of delight,
Softest clothing, woolly, bright; ...
Little Lamb, who made thee?
Dost thou know who made thee?

Little Lamb, I'll tell thee,
Little Lamb, I'll tell thee:
He is called by thy name,
For He calls Himself a lamb,
He is meek, and He is mild;
He became a little child.
I a child, and thou a lamb,
We are called by His name.
Little Lamb, God bless thee!
Little Lamb, God bless thee!"

O Lord, Lamb of God, holy Christ-Child, You Who are Love-come-down-from-Heaven above, accept the imperfect love we offer. Help us to become gentle, meek and mild. Deepen our perception of You; strengthen our ability to truly love, we pray, and let it flow freely to others as Your great compassion poured over the earth and all its peoples when You became the perfect Paschal Lamb for us. Amen.

LAMB OF THE LAMB (28)

Sleep on, O lamb of the Lamb, sleep on:
And may His angels guard, protect you,
With their shimmering wings enfold you,

Tenderly love, tenderly hold you;
O lamb of the Lamb, sleep on.

Dream on, O lamb of the Lamb, dream on;
Dream of the Christ-Child's heavenly birthday,
Presents, toys, love and child-play,
Happy people all through that day,
O lamb of the Lamb, dream on.

Sleep on, O lamb of the Lamb, sleep on;
And when it comes that you must wake
And grow to manhood -- don't forsake
All He'd ask of your life to make
But for now, O little lamb, sleep on.

THE THIRD DAY OF CHRISTMAS

Luke 2: 12 - 14

Again, the angels, God's messengers, herald the magnificent birth, singing *"Glory to God in the highest."*

"'This will be a sign to you: You will find a baby wrapped in cloths and lying in a manger.' Suddenly a great company of the heavenly host appeared with the angel, praising God and saying,
'Glory to God in the highest, and on earth peace ... .'"

Luke 2: 12 - 14

Throughout the annals of time, angels have borne awesome news. During that first Christmas, angels spoke many times: they spoke to Zechariah, to Mary, to Joseph (repeatedly), to the shepherds and to the Wise Men. They bore good tidings, advised, and warned. They were doubted, questioned, feared and wondered about. Often, the key words they used were: "... *listen!*" and "... *do not be afraid."*

It is a thing to wonder about -- how many times we may have been warned, advised, comforted or greeted in some way by angels of whose presence we've been unaware -- angels who have urged us to *"Listen!"* to God's message, and *"... do not be afraid"* for He is with us.

Lord, our Good Shepherd, how can we thank You -- You who send us angels to guard, guide, protect and warn us? Grant us the ears to hear them, the eyes to see, and the heart and mind to understand their advice and direction. You, Who are all-glorious and all-loving -- You Who came down to live among us, forgive our sins and let us draw closer to You, now and always. Amen.

O LITTLE TOWN OF BETHLEHEM (29)

O little town of Bethlehem,
How still we see thee lie!
Above thy deep and dreamless sleep
The silent stars go by;
Yet in thy dark streets shineth
The everlasting Light;
The hopes and fears of all the years
Are met in thee tonight.

For Christ is born of Mary,
And gathered all above,
While mortals sleep, the angels keep
Their watch of wondering love.
O morning stars together
Proclaim the holy birth!
And praises sing to God the King,
And peace to men on earth.

How silently, how silently,
The wondrous gift is given!
So God imparts to human hearts
The blessings of His heaven.
No ear may hear His coming,
But in this world of sin,
Where meek souls will receive Him, still
The dear Christ enters in.

O holy Child of Bethlehem!
Descend to us, we pray;
Cast out our sin and enter in,
Be born in us today.
We hear the Christmas angels
The glad tidings tell;
O come to us, abide with us,
Our Lord, Emmanuel! Amen.

by Phillips Brooks (Bishop)[14]

THE FOURTH DAY OF CHRISTMAS

Luke 2: 15 & 16

After the angels appeared to the shepherds, they hurried to Bethlehem to see the wondrous thing that had happened.

"When the angels had left them and gone into heaven, the shepherds said to one another, 'Let's go to Bethlehem and see this thing that has happened, which the Lord has told us about.' So they hurried off and found Mary and Joseph, and the baby, who was lying in the manger."

Luke 2: 15 & 16

When the shepherds, filled with wonder and awe, went to the small stable stall, they found the holy Infant:

INFANT HOLY (30)

"Infant holy, infant lowly,
For his bed a cattle stall;
Oxen lowing, little knowing
Christ the babe is Lord of all.
Swift are winging, angels singing,

---

[14] The Reverend Philips Brooks, an Episcopal Bishop in Boston, has been called "the greatest American preacher of the 19th century." He is also noted for his efforts on behalf of abolition and of granting voting rights to former slaves.

Nowells ringing, tidings bringing:
Christ the babe is Lord of all!
Christ the babe is Lord of all!"

Polish carol

Lord Jesus, holy Child of Bethlehem, cast out our sin, *"be born in us today."* Dearest Christ-Child, born for shepherds and for kings -- for the low and for the high -- have mercy on us. Bless all those who seek You and have lost their way; bless those we love and those we have difficulty loving; guide us by Your holy Light home to be with You forever. Amen.

JOSEPH DEAREST (31)

"Joseph dearest, Joseph mine,
Help me cradle this Child divine;
God reward thee and all that's thine
In Paradise,"
So prays the mother Mary.

He came among us at Christmastide,
At Christmastide,
In Bethlehem;
Men shall bring Him from far and wide
Love's diadem:
Jesus, Jesus,
Lo, He comes, and loves, and saves, and frees us!

"Gladly, dear one, lady mine,
Help I cradle this Child of thine;
God's own light on us both shall shine
In Paradise,
As prays the mother Mary."

German carol ca. 1500[15]

---

[15] This German Carol dates possibly from as early as the 14th century. First sung in Latin as "Resonet in Laudibus," it was later sung as a lullaby by Mary in religious plays performed near Leipzig, Germany.

THE FIFTH DAY OF CHRISTMAS

Luke 2: 17 - 18

What wonder and awe transpired around Jesus' birth!

"When they had seen him, they spread the word concerning what had been told them about this child, and all who heard it were amazed at what the shepherds said to them."

Luke 2: 17 - 18

The shepherds were at first frightened, then astonished, then filled with the joy the angels promised. Imagine the amazement of those to whom the shepherds told their story.

Christina Rossetti, the British poet, described what she would have brought the Lamb of God.

> "What can I give Him, (32)
> Poor as I am?
> If I were a shepherd
> I would give a lamb.
> If I were a wise man,
> I would do my part,
> Yet what can I give Him?
> Give my heart."

Lord Jesus, we give You our hearts. Amen.

IT CAME UPON A MIDNIGHT CLEAR (33)

> It came upon a midnight clear,
> That glorious song of old,
> For angels bending down to earth
> To touch their harps of gold:
> "Peace on the earth, good will to men,
> From heaven's all-gracious King."
> The world in solemn stillness lay
> To hear the angels sing.

Still through the cloven skies they came
With peaceful wings unfurled,
And still their heavenly music floats
O'er all the weary world.
Above its sad and lonely plains
They bend in hovering wing,
And ever o'er its Babel-sounds
The blessed angels sing.

Yet with the woes of sin and strife
The world has suffered long;
Beneath the heavenly strain have rolled
Two thousand years of wrong;
And man, at war with man, hears not
The tidings which they bring;
O hush the noise, ye men of strife,
And hear the angels sing!

O ye, beneath life's crushing load,
Whose forms are bending low,
We toil along the climbing way
With painful steps and slow.
Look now! for glad and golden hours
Come softly on the wing;
O rest beside the weary road
And hear the angels sing!

For lo! the days are hastening on,
By prophets seen of old,
When the ever-circling years
Shall come the time foretold,
When peace shall over all the earth
Its ancient splendors fling,
And the whole world give back the song
Which now the angels sing.

Edmund H. Sears 1849[16]

---

[16] Edmund Hamilton Sears, a young Harvard educated Unitarian minister, wrote this hymn while sitting in his New England study on a cold winter's day.

THE SIXTH DAY OF CHRISTMAS

Luke 2: 20; Psalm 23

As the shepherds left the stable, glorifying and praising God, the Holy Family rested, surrounded by this marvelous radiance of wonder, peace and joy.

> *"The shepherds returned, glorifying and praising God for all the things they had heard and seen, which were just as they had been told."*
>
> Luke 2: 20

When thinking of the shepherds at Jesus' birth, one is reminded of the beloved Shepherd Psalm, a gift that has given comfort, peace and joy to countless numbers of people since it was written thousands of years ago:

> *"The Lord is my shepherd; I shall not be in want.*
> *He makes me lie down in green pastures,*
> *he leads me beside quiet waters.*
> *he restores my soul;*
> *He guides me in paths of righteousness for his name's sake.*
> *Even though I walk through the valley of the shadow of death,*
> *I will fear no evil, for you are with me;*
> *your rod and your staff,*
> *they comfort me.*
> *You prepare a table before me in the presence of my enemies.*
> *You anoint my head with oil;*
> *my cup overflows.*
> *Surely goodness and love will follow me all the days of my life;*
> *and I will dwell in the house of the Lord forever. Amen."*
>
> Psalm 23

There is an old French Christmas carol about angels. A story tells that on Christmas Eve, French shepherds have sung this ancient hymn to each other, resounding the words from hills and mountains across fields and valleys *"echoing their joyous strains."*

ANGELS WE HAVE HEARD ON HIGH (34)

"Angels we have heard on high,
Sweetly singing o'er the plains,
And the mountains in reply,
Echoing their joyous strains.
Gloria in excelsis Deo.

Shepherds, why this jubilee?
Why your joyous strains prolong?
What the gladsome tidings be
Which inspire your heav'nly song?
Gloria in excelsis Deo.

Come to Bethlehem and see
Him whose birth the angels sing;
Come adore on bended knee.
Christ the Lord, the newborn King.
Gloria in excelsis Deo."

Dear holy Shepherd-King, You Who were born in a stable in Bethlehem to lead Your people safely home to You -- lead us still. May we always be counted among Your flock. Restore our souls. By Your grace, allow us to walk within Your pleasant pastures, drink of the water that quenches all thirst, and be with You always, now and forevermore. Amen.

JOY TO THE WORLD (35)

Joy to the world! the Lord is come:
Let earth receive her King;
Let every heart prepare Him room,
And heaven and nature sing.

Joy to the world! the savior reigns;
Let men their songs employ,
While fields and floods, rocks, hills and plains,
Repeat the sounding joy.

No more let sins and sorrows grow,
Nor thorns infest the ground;
He comes to make His blessings flow
Far as the curse is found.

He rules the world with truth and grace,
And makes the nations prove
The glories of His righteousness,
And wonders of His love.

Isaac Watts 1719[17]

THE SEVENTH DAY OF CHRISTMAS

Luke 2: 25 – 35

Simeon, who had been promised by the Holy Spirit that he would not die until he had seen the Lord Christ, felt prompted to go to the temple the same time that Joseph and Mary went there with Baby Jesus.

"Now there was a man in Jerusalem called Simeon, who was righteous and devout. He was waiting for the consolation of Israel, and the Holy Spirit was upon him. It had been revealed to him by the Holy Spirit that he would not die before he had seen the Lord's Christ. Moved by the Spirit, he went into the temple courts. When the parents brought in the child Jesus to do for him what the custom of the law required, Simeon took him in his arms and praised God, saying:
'Sovereign Lord, as you have promised,
you now dismiss your servant in peace.
For my eyes have seen your salvation,
which you have prepared in the sight of all people, a light for revelation to the Gentiles
and for the glory to your people Israel.'
The child's father and mother marveled at what was said about him. Then Simeon blessed them and said to Mary, his mother:

---

[17] Considered the Father of English Hymnology, Isaac Watts wrote over 600 hymns. "Joy to the World" is based on the 98th Psalm and was first published in 1719 in a collection of his poems entitled *Psalms of David*.

'This child is destined to cause the falling and rising of many in Israel, and to be a sign that will be spoken against, so that the thoughts of many hearts will be revealed. And a sword will pierce your own soul, too.'"

Luke 2: 25 – 35

Simeon immediately knew Jesus and took the Baby into his arms, praising God and prophesying. What a time of joy for Simeon! What a time of wonder for Joseph and Mary!

O Lord, You Who are, as Simeon said, *"..a light for revelation to the Gentiles and for the glory to your people... ,"*
light our paths through the night of our life here on earth. You Who became a sign rejected, reject us not. Cleanse us so that we may draw ever closer to You. Accept, through Jesus' sake, our imperfect love, and hold us among Your own, now and always. Amen.

THE SONG (36)

Why do the bells of Christmas ring?
Why do little children sing?
Once a lovely shining star,
Seen by shepherds from afar,
Gently moved until its light
Made a manger's cradle bright.

There a darling baby lay,
Pillowed soft upon the hay,
And its mother sang and smiled:
"This is Christ, the Holy Child."
Therefore the bells for Christmas ring.
Therefore the little children sing.

Eugene Field 1850 - 1895[18]

---

[18] Eugene Field, nineteenth century poet who began his writing career as a newspaper columnist in St. Louis, wrote many poems for children.

THE EIGHTH DAY OF CHRISTMAS

Luke 2: 21 - 24; Matthew 1: 21

And so, as the angel told them, Mary and Joseph on the eighth day, the day of circumcision, named the Child Jesus. The angel said to give Him this name.

"On the eighth day, when it was time to circumcise him, he was named Jesus, the name the angel had given him before he had been conceived. When the time of their purification according to the Law of Moses had been completed, Joseph and Mary took him to Jerusalem to present him to the Lord (as it is written in the Law of the Lord. 'Every firstborn male is to be consecrated to the Lord'), and to offer a sacrifice in keeping with what is said in the Law of the Lord: 'a pair of doves or two young pigeons.'"

Luke 2: 21 - 24

"She will give birth to a son, and you are to give him the name Jesus, because he will save his people from their sins."

Matthew 1: 21

He was the Hope of mankind for all time, this everlasting Light, this Christ-Child born in Bethlehem. After being circumcised and named, Mary and Joseph took Jesus to Jerusalem to be consecrated.

Lord Jesus, on this, the eighth day of Christmas and the first day of the new year, let us, too, be made new through the graciousness of You Who came to earth in newness and Light. Amen.

THE NINTH DAY OF CHRISTMAS

Luke 2: 36 - 38

There was Anna -- another godly person -- who on seeing Jesus, praised God; she was another who knew who He was, even as an Infant-Child.

"There was also a prophetess, Anna, the daughter of Phanuel, of the tribe of Asher. She was very old; she had lived with her husband seven years after her marriage, and then was a widow until she was eighty-four. She never left

the temple but worshipped night and day, fasting and praying. Coming up to them at that very moment, she gave thanks to God and spoke about the child to all who were looking forward to the redemption of Jerusalem."

Luke 2: 36 - 38

Imagine how Mary and Joseph wondered at those who recognized their divine Son. How they must have pondered and treasured all this in their hearts! First there were the angels, then there was Elizabeth, then there were the shepherds, the kings, Simeon and now Anna, the widowed prophetess who spent her time in fasting and prayer.

All of these knew "What Child is this?"

"What Child is this, who, laid to rest, (37)
On Mary's lap is sleeping?
Whom angels greet with anthems sweet,
While shepherds watch are keeping?

This, this is Christ the King,
Whom shepherds guard and angels sing:
Haste, haste to bring Him laude,
The Babe, the Son of Mary.

Why lies He in such mean estate
Where ox and ass are feeding?
Good Christian, fear: for sinners here
The silent Word is pleading.

This, this is Christ the King,
Whom shepherds guard and angels sing:
Haste, haste to bring Him laud,
The Babe, the Son of Mary.

So bring Him incense, gold and myrrh,
Come peasant, king, to own Him,
The King of kings salvation brings,
Let loving hearts enthrone Him."

William C. Dix [19]

---

[19] William Chatterton Dix, a 19th century British poet, was especially fond of writing of the wonder of God. Over forty of his poems are now hymns.

O Lord, Christ-the-King Who came as a tiny Child, hear our prayer. Forgive our sin and enter in; fill our lives with the sweetness of Your Being. Let us never fail to recognize You -- never fail to bring You praise and adoration. Help us to see You in everyone we meet, sharing the love You shared so freely. Amen.

FROM THE SECOND CANON OF COSMAS OF MAIUMA (38)

"Of old the Master that works wonders saved His people, making the watery wave of the sea into dry land; and now of His own will has He been born from a maiden, and so He established a path for us whereby we may mount to heaven. We glorify Him who in essence is equal to the Father and to mortal men.
Glory be to Thee, our God, glory to Thee.
Plainly foreshadowed by the burning bush that was not consumed, a hallowed womb has borne the Word. God is mingled with the form of mortal men, and so He looses the unhappy womb of Eve from the bitter curse of old. We men give Him glory.
Glory be to Thee, our God, glory to Thee.
A star shown plainly to the Magi the Word that was before the sun, Who has come to make transgression cease. They saw Thee wrapped in swaddling clothes, within a poor and lowly cave, Who sharest all our sufferings, and in joy they gazed upon Thee, Who art at once both man and Lord."

THE TENTH DAY OF CHRISTMAS

Matthew 2: 1-6; Isaiah 60: 6

Wise men in the east saw a magnificent star as it rose. By the grace of God, in their wisdom, they knew that it would direct them to *"where the Christ was to be born."*

"After Jesus was born in Bethlehem in Judea, during the time of King Herod, Magi from the east came to Jerusalem and asked, 'Where is the one who has

been born king of the Jews? We saw his star in the east and have come to worship him.' When King Herod heard this he was disturbed, and all Jerusalem with him. When he had called together all the people's chief priests and teachers of the law, he asked them where the Christ was to be born. 'In Bethlehem in Judea,' they replied, 'for this is what the prophet has written:
'But you, Bethlehem, in the land of Judah,
are by no means least among the rulers of Judah;
for out of you will come a ruler who will be the shepherd of my people Israel.'"

Matthew 2: 1-6

When the Wise Men arrived in Jerusalem inquiring of this, King Herod was disturbed that someone might usurp his power. His scribes and chief priests quoted to Herod what the prophets had said hundreds of years earlier.

Among the many Old Testament prophecies that point to the Wise Men's visit to Christ is this one by Isaiah:

*"Herds of camels will cover your land,
young camels of Midian and Ephah.
And all from Sheba will come,
bearing gold and incense
and proclaiming the praise of the Lord."*

Isaiah 60: 6

Dear Lord Jesus, in remembering the Wise Men bringing their gifts to You, and in trying to comprehend this most magnificent, unspeakably wonderful Gift You gave to us, help us to always, at all times, realize that whatever gifts we may have are not and never have been of our doing, but Yours. Help us to use them in some way for You, which is only to return to You what is, always was and always will be Yours. May we, in whatever way possible, use Your gifts to Your glory. Amen.

WE THREE KINGS (39)

We three kings of Orient are,
Bearing gifts, we traverse afar,
Field and fountain,
Moor and mountain,
Following yonder star.
O star of wonder, star of night,
Star with royal beauty bright;
Westward leading,
Still proceeding,
Guide us to thy perfect light!

(Gaspar)   Born a King on Bethlehem's plain,
Gold I bring to crown Him again,
King forever,
Ceasing never
Over us all to reign.
O star of wonder, star of night,
Westward leading,
Still proceeding,
Guide us to that perfect light!

(Melchoir)   Frankincense to offer have I,
Incense owns a Deity nigh,
Prayer and praising,
All men raising,
Worship Him God on high.
O star of wonder, star of night,
Westward leading,
Still proceeding,
Guide us to thy perfect light!

(Balthazar)   Myrrh is mine; its bitter perfume
Breathes a life of gathering gloom;
Sorrow, sighing,
Bleeding, dying,

Sealed in the stone-cold tomb.
O star of wonder, star of night,
Westward leading,
Still proceeding,
Guide us to thy perfect light!

John H. Hopkins, Jr. [20]

THE ELEVENTH DAY OF CHRISTMAS

Isaiah 60:1 - 3; Psalm 72: 10; Matthew 2: 7 - 12

Both the Old and the New Testaments tell of the coming of the Magi to see the newborn Christ.

*"Arise, shine, for your light has come,
and the glory of the Lord rises upon you.
See, darkness covers the earth
and thick darkness is over the peoples,
but the Lord rises upon you
and his glory appears over you.
Nations will come to your light,
and kings to the brightness of your dawn.."*

Isaiah 60: 1 - 3

"The kings of Tarshish and of distant shores will bring tribute to him; the kings of Sheba and Seba will present him with gifts."

Psalm 72: 10

"Then Herod called the Magi secretly and found out from them the exact time the star had appeared. He sent them to Bethlehem and said, 'Go and make a careful search for the child. As soon as you find him, report to me, so that I too may go and worship him.' After they had heard the king, they went on their way, and the star they had seen in the east went ahead of them until it was stopped over the place where the child was. When they saw the star they were overjoyed. On coming to the house, they saw the child with his

---

[20] In 1857, the Reverend John Henry Hopkins, Jr. wrote both the words and the music for the popular Advent carol "We Three Kings" to be used in a Christmas pageant for the General Theological Seminary in New York City.

mother Mary, and they bowed down and worshipped him. Then they opened their treasures and presented him with gifts of gold and incense and myrrh. And having been warned in a dream not to go back to Herod, they returned to their country by another route."

Matthew 2: 7 - 12

Although sometimes called Magi, and sometimes Wise Men (the Greek derivative word "major" is closely translated as those highly learned in the arts and sciences), Old Testament prophets prophesied many times of these regal visitors, speaking of them in many translations as wise kings. The Holy Scriptures never mention their number, and in the early days they were sometimes spoken of as more than three. Possibly because of their three gifts they came to be known as "The Three Kings."

The gifts of gold, frankincense and myrrh represent three attributes of Christ -- as king, high priest and physician -- the divine tri-fold holy God-Gift to the world at Christmas.

The Magi brought these gifts. But what can we give Him?

"During this memorable night, each creature hastened to bring its gift to the Saviour-King:
heaven-- a star;
the earth -- a cave;
the wilderness -- a manger;
the angels -- singing;
the shepherds -- worship;
the Magi -- gifts.
Therefore, we too should not come to Him "empty-handed," but should bring Him what is more valuable than anything else -- our pure, believing hearts. For the high God has appeared on earth, in order to raise us up to heaven!"
(40)

Dear beloved Christ-Child, our King, Priest and Physician, You Who came down at Christmas as Love incarnate, encompass us in the warm wreath of Your eternal care. Help us to be able to bring to You "our pure, believing hearts." Amen.

THE THREE KINGS (41)

Three kings came riding from far away,
Melchior and Gasper and Baltazar;
Three wise men out of the east were they
And they traveled by night and slept by day.
For their guide was a beautiful, wonderful star.

Three caskets they bore on their saddle-bows,
Three caskets of gold with golden keys;
Their robes were of crimson silk with rows
Of bells and pomegranates and furbelows,
Their turbans like blossoming almond-trees.

And the three kings rode through the gate and the guard,
Through the silent street, 'till their horses turned
And neighed as they entered the great in-yard;
But the windows were closed and the gates were barred,
And only a light in the stable burned.

And cradled there in the scented hay,
In the air made sweet by the breath of kine,
The little Child in the manger lay,
The Child that would be king one day
Of a kingdom not human but divine.

His mother Mary of Nazareth
Sat watching beside His place of rest,
Watching the even flow of His breath,
For the joy of life and the terror of death
Were mingled together in her breast.

They laid their offerings at His feet
The gold was their tribute to a King.
The frankincense, with its odor sweet,
Was for the Priest, the Paraclete
The myrrh for the body's burying.

       Henry Wadsworth Longfellow[21]

---

[21] Henry Wadsworth Longfellow, the prominent 19th century poet and descendent of New England Puritans, wrote with deep feeling, empathy and understanding.

TWELFTH DAY OF CHRISTMAS
THEOPHANY, EPIPHANY AND THREE KINGS DAY

Mark 1: 7 & 8; Matthew 3: 13-17; Isaiah 60: 1; Psalm 46:1

Today, January 6, is observed in the East as Theophany (manifestation of God), in the west as Epiphany, and in many (especially Latin) countries, this is the traditional Three Kings Day when gifts are shared in memory of the gifts they brought to the Christ-Child. Among Roman Catholics in the United States, Epiphany is celebrated on a Sunday near January 6th.

As Theophany/Epiphany/Three Kings Day, this day celebrates the public manifestation of God. His miraculous manifestation to the Magi represents the revelation of Jesus to the Gentiles. The manifestation of the Holy Trinity came when Jesus was baptized by John who once said:

"After me will come one more powerful than I, the thongs of whose sandals I am not worthy to stoop down and untie. I baptize you with water, but he will baptize you with the Holy Spirit."

Mark 1: 7 & 8

Jesus came to the River Jordan while John was preaching and baptizing. This could have been near the Dead Sea, the lowest place on earth. It would be significant that Jesus began His ministry there, coming from the highest place to the very lowest, before finally ascending once again.

"Then Jesus came from Galilee to the Jordan to be baptized by John. But John tried to deter him, saying, 'I need to be baptized by you, and do you come to me?' Jesus replied, 'Let it be so now; it is proper for us to do this to fulfill all righteousness.' Then John consented. As soon as Jesus was baptized, he went up out of the water. At that moment heaven was opened, and he saw the Spirit of God descending like a dove and lighting on him. And a voice from heaven said, 'This is my Son, whom I love, with him I am well pleased.'"

Matthew 3: 13-17

The most marvelous, wondrous happening! Here was Jesus -- God the Son -- standing in the water after being immersed in the River Jordan by the fore-runner John; heaven opened and here was God the Father's voice speaking from there: *"This is my Son, whom I love, with him I am well pleased."* And here was the Holy Spirit descending like a dove from Paradise to Jesus, on earth, in our very midst.

The incomprehensible mystery was made known, that here, indeed, was God in three persons -- the Father, Son and Holy Spirit -- revealed suddenly and unexpectedly, as His second coming will also be. This Trinity that was described so aptly by St. Patrick in the symbolism of the clover-leaf -- one, indivisible, yet with three distinct yet equal parts.

Epiphany can also symbolize a tri-fold manifestation of Jesus: to the Magi (Gentiles); in His baptism when the Father and Holy Spirit were evident; and in Christ's miracles.

Again, a prophecy of Isaiah:

*"Arise, shine, for your light has come,
and the glory of the Lord rises upon you."*

Isaiah 60:1

God the Father, God the Son, and God the Holy Spirit, by Your infinite mercy and boundless Love made manifest among us, forgive our sins and hear our prayer. You Who came to earth in utmost humility as an Infant-Child that we might have life, teach us to share Your love and mercy, and to know and do Your will in this life, enfold us in Your Love and guide us home to live with You forevermore. Amen.

GIOVANNI'S GIFTS (42)

There is nothing I can give you
which you have not; but there is much, very much,
that, while I cannot give it, you can take.

No heaven can come to us unless our hearts
find rest in today. Take heaven!
No peace lies in the future which is not hidden
in the present. Take peace!

The gloom of the world is but a shadow.
Behind it, yet within our reach, is joy. Take joy!
There is radiance and glory in the darkness
could we but see it, and to see, we have only to look.
I beseech you to look.

Life is so generous a giver, but we,
judging the gifts by the covering,
cast them away as ugly, or heavy, or hard.
Know the covering, and you will find beneath it,
a living splendor, woven of love, by wisdom, with power.

Welcome it, grasp it, and you touch the
angel's hand that brings it to you.
Everything we call a trial, a sorrow, or a duty,
believe me, that angel's hand is there;
the gift is there,
and the wonder of an overshadowing presence.
Our joy's too; be not content with them as joys.
They, too, conceal diviner gifts.

Life is full of meaning and purpose,
so full of beauty -- beneath its covering --
that you will find earth but cloaks your heaven.

Courage then to claim it; that is all!
But courage you have; and the knowledge that we
are pilgrims together,
wending through unknown country, home.

And so, at this Christmas time, I greet you
Not quite as the world sends greetings,
but with profound esteem and with the prayer
that for you, now and forever,
the day breaks and the shadows flee away.

Fra Giovanni December 1513[22]

---

[22] A letter of advice written to a wealthy contessina from a 16th century Italian monk.

REFERENCES/ENDNOTES

1. THE HOLY BIBLE: NEW INTERNATIONAL VERSION, (Colorado Springs: International Bible Society, (c) 1994) (All Biblical quotes in this book are from this version of the Holy Bible and used by permission.)
2. William Duranti, rpt in HANDBOOK OF CHRISTIAN FEASTS AND CUSTOMS, Francis X. Weiser, (New York: Harcourt, Brace & World, Inc., (c) 1958), p. 53.
3. Emily Chisholm, "The Holly and the Ivy," HYMNS & PSALMS, printed by permission of Hope Publishing Company, (London: Methodist Publishing House, (c) 1983), #88.
4. Alexander Men, SON OF MAN, trans. Samuel Brown, Previously published in 1992 in Russia as SYN CHELOVECHECHESKII, (Torrence, California: Oakwood Publications, (c)1998), p. 219.
5. Christina Georgina Rossetti, "Advent," THE POETICAL WORKS OF CHRISTINA GEORGINA ROSSETTI, (London: Macmillan and Company, Ltd., (c) 1928), p. 148.
6. Cosmas of Maiuma, CANON OF COSMAS OF MAIUMA, ODE THREE, in "The Nativity of Christ," Bishop Alexander Mileant, (Los Angeles: Holy Protection Russian Orthodox Church, 1997), p. 12.
7. John Wesley, "Come Thou Long Expected Jesus," SERVICE BOOK AND HYMNAL, (Minneapolis: Augsburg Publishing House, (c) 1958), p. 5.
8. Alexander Men, SON OF MAN, pp. 26 & 27.
9. "Veni Emmanuel," ancient French carol, trans. John Mason Neale, THE HYMNAL (Plimpton, Massachusetts: Plimpton Press, (c) 1940), p. 2.
10. By author, "Little Jesus," *The Companion,* December, 1996, p. 17.

11. "God be in My Head," from Sarum Primer, rpt. in THE HYMNAL, p. 466.
12. Charles Coffin, "On Jordan's Banks," THE HYMNAL, p.10.
13. "Agnus Dei," SAINT JOSEPH DAILY MISSAL (New York: Catholic Book Publishing Company, (c) 1959), p. 689.
14. "A Rose-Tree," 16th century German carol taken from the eleventh chapter of Isaiah 11, THE HYMNAL, p. 17.
15. By author, "Legend of the Holly," *The Companion,* December, (c) 1992, p. 17.
16. Virgil, ECOLOGUE IV, trans. John Dryden, VIRGIL IN ENGLISH, (London: Penguin Books, Ltd., (c) 1996), p. 139.
17. Author unknown
18. Richard of Chichester, THE HYMNAL, p. 429.
19. Alfred Lord Tennyson, excerpted from poem "Passing of Arthur" in IDOLS OF THE KING, (New York: Heritage Press, (c) 1939), p. 285.
20. Alexander Men, SON OF MAN, p. 220.
21. John Betjeman, excerpted from poem "Christmas," in COLLECTED POEMS OF JOHN BETJEMAN, (Boston: Houghton Mifflin Company, (c) 1971), p. 190.
22. Cosmas of Maiuma, CANON OF COSMAS OF MAIUMA, ODE ONE, in "The Nativity of Christ," Alexander Mileant, p. 11.
23. Rossetti, excerpted from "Christmas Eve," POETICAL WORKS, p. 158..
24. Placide Cappeau De Roquemaure, trans. John S. Dwight, ed. Shane Weller, CHRISTMAS CAROLS, (New York: Dover Publications, Inc., (c) 1992), p. 41.
25. Rossetti, "Love Came Down at Christmas," POETICAL WORKS, p. 159.
26. Joseph Mohr, THE HYMNAL, p. 33.
27. William Blake, ADVENTURES IN ENGLISH LITERATURE, (New York: Harcourt Brace & Company, (c) 1958), p. 330.
28. Author, "lamb of the Lamb," *Wesleyan Advocate,* December, 1986, p. 11, rpt. in *Nazareth,* December, (c) 1995, p. 31.
29. Phillips Brooks, SERVICE BOOK AND HYMNAL, (Minneapolis: Augsburg Publishing House, (c) 1958), p. 27.
30. "Infant Holy, infant lowly", Polish folk song, FOLKSONGS FROM EASTERN EUROPE, (London: Faber Music, Ltd., (c) 1992), p. 29.
31. "Joseph Dearest, Joseph Mine," ancient German carol, THE HYMNAL, p. 45.

32. Christina Rossetti, excerpted from poem "A Christmas Carol," WHAT CAN I GIVE HIM, (New York: Holiday House, (c) 1998), pp. 15 - 24.
33. Edmund Hamilton Sears, SERVICE BOOK AND HYMNAL, p. 19.
34. "Angels We have Heard on High," traditional French carol, trans. James Chadwick, THE HYMNAL, p. 42.
35. Isaac Watts, SERVICE BOOK AND HYMNAL, p. 15.
36. Eugene Field, "The Song," (New York: Charles Scribner's Sons, (c) 1949) p. 532.
37. William Chatterton Dix, THE HYMNAL, p. 36.
38. Cosmas of Maiuma, "The Nativity of Christ," Bishop Alexander Mileant, P. 11.
39. John Henry Hopkins, Jr., "We Three Kings", THE HYMNAL, p. 51.
40. From an English interpretation of the Christmas service of the Orthodox Church, as excerpted from "The Nativity of Christ," ed. and trans. Bishop Alexander Mileant, p. 17, derived from work by Anatolius in Seraphim Nassar, DIVINE PRAYERS AND SERVICES OF THE CATHOLIC ORTHODOX CHURCH OF CHRIST (Englewood, NJ: Antiochian Orthodox Christian Archdiocese of North America, (c) 1979) p. 397.
41. Henry Wadsworth Longfellow, "The Three Kings", THE COMPLETE POETICAL WORKS OF LONGFELLOW, (Cutchogue, New York: Houghton Mifflin, (c) 1993), p. 339.
42. "Fra Giovanni's Gifts," HOME BOOK OF CHRISTMAS, ed. May L. Becker, (New York: Dodd, Mead, (c) 1941), pp. 636 & 637.